Data Stewardship in Practice

From Policies to People, From Roles to Results

Dave Wells

Technics Publications
SEDONA, ARIZONA

TECHNICS PUBLICATIONS

115 Linda Vista, Sedona, AZ 86336 USA
https://www.TechnicsPub.com

Edited by Steve Hoberman
Cover design by Lorena Molinari

First Printing 2025

Copyright © 2025 by Dave Wells

ISBN, print ed.   9798898160258
ISBN, Kindle ed.   9798898160265
ISBN, PDF ed.   9798898160272

Library of Congress Control Number: 2025947223

Contents

How to Use This Book

Data Stewardship in Practice is not a book meant to be read cover to cover. It is designed as a reference that different readers can approach in different ways, depending on their role, responsibilities, and immediate needs. Use it as a guidebook, the sections you turn to first will depend on who you are and what you need to accomplish:

- **Data Stewards**: Start with Chapter 1 to ground your understanding of stewardship principles. Chapters 3, 4, and 5 provide the details of roles, knowledge areas, and problem-solving approaches. Keep the Appendix handy as a quick reference when facing real-world issues.

- **Data Governors and Councils**: Chapters 2 and 6 are especially relevant, covering stewardship structures, governance alignment, and program evolution.

- **Program Leaders and Sponsors (CDO, CIO, and Business Executives)**: Chapter 6 should be your starting point, with its emphasis on sponsorship, metrics, maturity, and roadmaps. Chapters 1 and 2 provide critical context.

- **Business and Functional Leaders**: Chapter 4 will help you see how stewardship connects to business functions, compliance, and day-to-day decision-making. Chapter 5 and the Appendix show how common problems can be diagnosed and resolved.

- **Supporting Roles (Architects, Data Managers, and Analysts)**: Chapters 4 and 5 are most relevant, with practical guidance on metadata, architecture, integration, and diagnostic techniques. Chapter 1 provides the shared concepts that link your work with stewardship.

While certain sections are written with particular roles in mind, every reader may find value in exploring beyond their immediate responsibilities. Stewards benefit from seeing how executives view sponsorship and governance. Leaders benefit from understanding the day-to-day challenges that stewards face. Architects and analysts benefit from recognizing how stewardship principles shape the use and management of data.

Understanding the perspectives and contributions of other roles is central to effective stewardship.

In this way, the book serves both as a targeted reference and as a shared resource for building mutual understanding across the stewardship community. By exploring chapters outside your direct focus, you gain a robust picture of the environment you work in, the challenges your colleagues face, and the ways stewardship fits together as a whole.

ONE

Data Stewardship Concepts

To understand data stewardship, it helps to begin with the underlying concept of stewardship.

> *Stewardship is the responsible and disciplined management of resources to ensure long-term benefit and stakeholder value.*

It is a principle that emphasizes sustainability, accountability, and care over time—not just operational efficiency in the short term. Stewardship applies across a wide range of domains: environmental, economic, technological, social, health, and cultural. In each case, the goal is the same: to manage resources in a way that preserves their value and utility for both current and future stakeholders.

Stewardship is built upon four key principles:

- Sustainability is the ability to maintain systems and processes over the long term, without depleting or damaging the resources they depend on. It's about building for durability and resilience.

- Conservation of resources is achieved through responsible resource management. Stewardship involves managing resources to keep them healthy, available, and fit for their intended purpose. This includes anticipating needs, monitoring use, and addressing issues before they become problems.

- Protection and Preservation are essential to safeguard resources from harm, degradation, or loss. This means taking proactive steps to identify risks, prevent damage, and ensure continuity.

- Advocacy and Engagement position the steward as a promoter and proponent for the value and responsible use of resources. This includes promoting policies, influencing culture, and engaging others in efforts to protect and improve the managed resources. These principles form the foundation of stewardship in any context.

What is Data Stewardship?

Now let's look specifically at stewardship of data—the responsible management of data throughout its lifecycle, from creation and collection to use, storage, and eventual disposal.

> *The top-level goals of data stewardship are to ensure data is understandable, accurate, accessible, and secure, and to ensure that data usage is ethical and compliant with legal and regulatory constraints.*

The principle of sustainability, when applied to data, focuses on the ability to maintain data management and consumption systems and processes over the long term without depleting or damaging the data resources upon which they depend. Conservation focuses on actively managing data resources to ensure their long-term health and to prevent misuse, depletion, degradation, corruption, and loss. Data protection safeguards data resources from harm, damage, and destruction, taking proactive measures to ensure preservation and mitigate potential threats and risks. Advocacy involves supporting and promoting data concepts, goals, and policies to bring about change, raise awareness, and foster data literacy—engaging others to drive positive business and data management outcomes.

Sustainability

Ability to maintain data management and consumption systems and processes over the long long term without depleting or damaging the data resources upon which they depend.

Conservation

Responsible management of data resources to ensure their long-term health and to prevent misuse, depletion, degradation, corruption, and loss of those resources.

Protection

Safeguarding and defending data resources from harm, damage and destruction – taking active measures to ensure preservation and to mitigate potential threats and risks.

advocacy

Supporting and promoting data concepts, goals and policies to bring about change, raise awareness, and foster data literacy – engaging others to drive positive business and data management outcomes.

Figure 1: What is Data Stewardship?

What is a Data Steward?

> *A Data Steward is an individual who takes responsibility for managing and overseeing how data is used across the organization.*

This is a governance role that focuses not just on the data itself, but also on how people access it, share it, protect it, and keep it useful and accurate. The definition highlights two key responsibilities: to perform the hands-on work of stewardship and to coordinate with a wide range of stakeholders: data owners, data consumers, data custodians, and others who rely on trusted data.

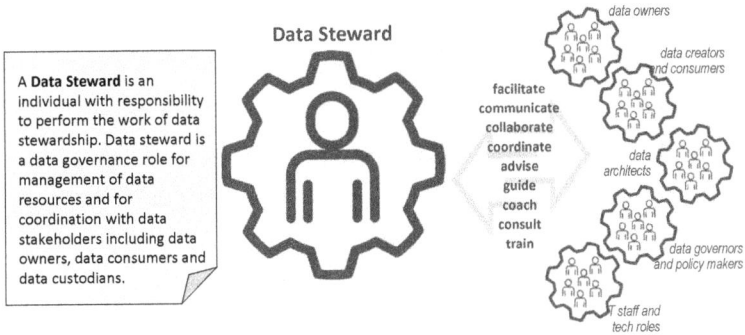

Figure 2: What is a Data Steward?

On the right side of this image, you see how data stewards connect with those stakeholders. A steward plays a central role in bringing together:

- Data Owners, who hold accountability for data
- Data Creators and Consumers, who generate and use data
- Data Architects, who design how data flows and is structured
- Policy Makers and Data Governors, who define rules
- IT and Tech Staff, who support the systems behind the data.

The steward doesn't just coordinate. They take action to:

- Facilitate, communicate, and collaborate across functions
- Coordinate activities

- Advise on decisions
- Guide, coach, consult, and train others in sound data practices.

This role is both strategic and operational. Data stewards help their organizations use data to create value, reduce risk, and build trust. They make sure the people, policies, and processes that surround data all move in the same direction.

The Role of Data Steward

Data steward is a role. It is not headcount, and it is not necessarily a designated position, a formal job title, or a full-time set of responsibilities. It is common for one individual to fill multiple roles. For example, a business analyst may also be a business unit data steward—two roles that are quite naturally compatible. It is also possible for one person to fill more than one data steward role, such as financial management business unit steward in combination with accounts payable process steward.

In most organizations, stewardship begins as a part-time responsibility assigned to subject matter experts or business analysts. As programs mature, dedicated full-time stewardship positions are likely to be created for critical data domains.

The role of Data Steward is often performed without having the formal job title. Many part-time stewards hold business titles such as Financial Analyst, Operations Manager, or other business functional titles. They take on stewardship responsibilities because they work with the data, and they have data subject expertise and a strong interest in responsible management of the data.

Kinds of Data Stewards

We'll look at five kinds of data stewards that are common in organizations. These aren't rigid categories—they're more like common patterns that reflect how organizations assign stewardship responsibilities. What really matters is the scope of work and the kind of data each steward focuses on.

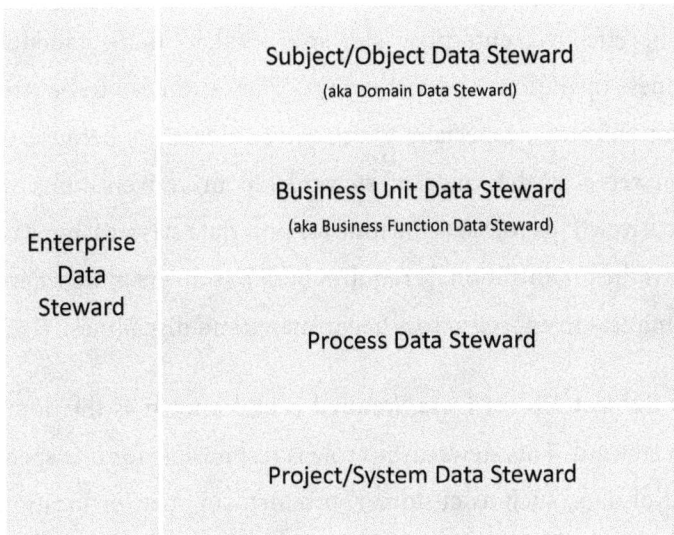

Figure 3: Kinds of Data Stewards.

The Enterprise Data Steward is usually the most senior and most strategic type of steward. Enterprise stewards look at the big picture. Their job is to oversee how data policies and standards apply across the entire organization. They don't just focus on one domain or system—they work to align all parts of the business around shared practices for managing and using data. One key responsibility is to coordinate the efforts of other stewards. Think of the enterprise steward as the lead or facilitator of the data stewardship team. They help bring together different perspectives—from business units, systems, and subject areas—to create consistency and alignment. This is a leadership position. It often involves setting direction for the whole stewardship program. Security, privacy, and compliance are common priorities, so enterprise stewards usually work closely with legal, risk, and compliance teams.

To be effective, enterprise stewards need to understand both business operations and technology. They also need to be strong communicators, especially with senior leadership, because they often serve as the voice of stewardship in conversations with executives. This role sets the tone for how data stewardship works across the organization. It requires both a strategic mindset and a willingness to engage across departments and disciplines.

The Subject/Object Data Steward is also known as the domain data steward. This stewardship role is responsible for one specific kind of data, such as customer, product, supplier, or location— any subject area that matters across systems and business processes. The key here is cross-functionality. A customer data steward, for example, might need to work with marketing, sales, billing, and customer support—because each of those areas collects and uses customer data in different ways. The goal is to make sure that the data stays consistent, reliable, and meaningful no matter where or how it's created, updated, and used. That includes reconciling differences, filling gaps, and sometimes negotiating trade-offs between business units. This role depends heavily on collaboration.

Subject stewards rely on input from subject matter experts in different departments, and they often coordinate closely with business unit, process, and system stewards. Data quality is a big focus—especially things like consistency across systems and agreement on standard definitions. To be effective, this kind of steward needs to be data literate and have some working knowledge of master data management and reference data management. They don't have to be technical experts, but they do need to understand the landscape of where and how their subject data appears. Think of this role as a connector that brings consistency to data that's used across the business, even when ownership and systems are distributed.

The Business Unit Data Steward role focuses on data within a single business area, such as finance, marketing, or HR. Their main responsibility is to manage the critical data that the unit creates and uses day to day. For example, a marketing data steward would look after campaign data, lead and contact data, and perhaps customer segmentation. A finance data steward might focus on accounts, budgets, and revenue data. These stewards serve as the data point of contact for their respective areas. They understand how the business uses the data, what makes it trustworthy, and where issues tend to show up. Because they work within a single function, they're deeply familiar with the business context. That means they can quickly spot problems that might not be obvious to someone outside the team—things like unexpected values, missing fields, and data that doesn't align with how the business actually works.

Business unit stewards are responsible for data quality within their scope. But they're also part of a bigger network. They're accountable to other stewards for the data their unit creates, and they rely on other stewards when their unit consumes data from somewhere else. This role requires strong domain knowledge, effective communication skills, and sufficient data literacy to apply best practices and assist the business in making informed use of its data. In many ways, this steward acts as a bridge between data and day-to-day operations. Their work ensures that the data their team depends on is both useful and dependable.

The Process Data Steward has responsibility for data that flows through an entire business process. This is different from stewarding data within a single team or department. Here, the focus is on how data moves across functions—through a complete workflow that usually involves multiple systems and business units. Think about something like order processing or product development. These processes often start in one part of the business and finish in another. Along the way, the data can pass through various departments, including marketing, sales, operations, logistics, and finance.

The process data steward tracks how the data changes and moves through stages and business units. They work to make sure the data remains accurate, consistent, and usable from start to finish. This involves working closely with business unit stewards to understand how each area interacts with the data, as well as with subject or object stewards to maintain domain-specific standards. This role requires a solid understanding of how the business process works—not just technically, but also operationally. The steward needs to know who does what, when it happens, and how each system and each business unit contributes to the overall flow. The data content often spans multiple subject areas. For example, recruiting-to-hiring involves candidate, position, interview, and onboarding data. The steward doesn't need to manage all of those subjects directly, but they do need to coordinate with the stewards who do. The data spans multiple domains. Take forecasting-to-budgeting, for instance. It pulls together revenue forecasts, cost estimates, financial plans, and performance metrics. One steward can't own all of that, but they play an important role in keeping the data aligned across finance, operations, and business units. This is an excellent role for someone who sees the big picture, understands the importance of handoffs, and knows how to bridge gaps between teams. It's all about maintaining data continuity and trust as the data moves through the organization.

The Project or System Data Steward works a little differently from the others. Instead of focusing on a domain, a department, or a business process, this steward focuses on the data inside one or more IT systems—or within the scope of a specific project. You'll often find this role involved in things like system implementations, data migrations, and major upgrades. They help define the data requirements for the system, advise on how to structure the data, and make sure it gets handled correctly throughout the project. For example, a system/project steward might be responsible for an electronic health records system or for a master data management platform. In both cases, the steward focuses on how the system handles data—not just what the data means, but how it's created, stored, protected, and moved from place to place. These stewards think about the technical side of data. They ask questions like:

- How is the data entered into the system?
- What happens to it when it's transformed or combined with other data?
- Where is it stored and who has access?
- How does the system protect sensitive data?
- How does that data get passed along to other systems or processes?

This role often bridges IT and business teams. The project or system data steward works closely with developers and system architects, but also needs to stay in sync with subject matter, business unit, and process stewards to ensure the system's data aligns with broader standards and expectations. This is an excellent fit for someone who is comfortable with both business needs and technical systems—someone who can effectively translate between business users and systems engineers, ensuring the data remains reliable throughout the system lifecycle.

> *Not every organization uses these titles. Some may combine roles or assign responsibilities a little differently. The key is to be clear about who's accountable for what and to ensure that stewardship roles align with the organization's priorities and resources. Also, the roles can evolve. As data needs change and as your stewardship efforts mature, it's perfectly normal for responsibilities to shift or expand.*

Who Becomes a Data Steward?

Data stewardship isn't a one-size-fits-all job and stewards don't all come from the same background. Instead, data stewards come from different parts of the organization, depending on the kind of stewardship role they take on.

Different types of professionals often step into each of the five steward roles. For example, enterprise stewards often come from a governance background. These are people who already work on policies, standards, and cross-functional coordination. But you might also see experienced data managers in this role, especially in organizations with mature data practices. Subject or domain stewards usually come from the business, where they've built deep knowledge about a specific kind of data. They might be business SMEs, data analysts, or data managers who understand both the details and the big picture. Business unit stewards often use data every day in their department. That could be someone in marketing operations, HR analytics, or financial reporting. These stewards usually start out as business users and become stewards because they understand how the team works with data—and where things can go wrong.

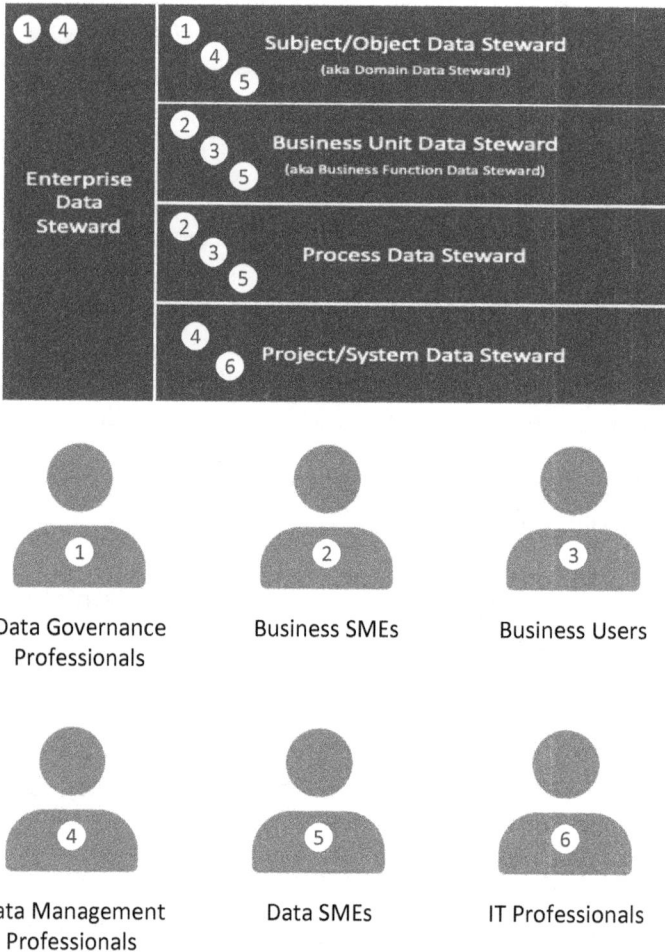

Figure 4: Who Becomes a Data Steward?

Process stewards need to understand how data flows across departments. That means they often come from roles like process improvement, business architecture, or cross-functional operations. They know how to follow the data across teams and spot breakdowns that others might miss. Project or system stewards tend to come from IT or system-specific roles. These might be data engineers, technical analysts, or system administrators who take on responsibility for how data is handled within a project or application.

So who becomes a data steward? It depends. What matters most is that the person understands the data in context, has credibility with their peers, and can help bridge gaps between people, systems, and expectations.

Characteristics of a Data Steward

What does it take to be a good data steward?
There's no single personality type or career path, but there are a few traits and qualities that tend to show up in effective stewards.

Let's start with personal traits. A steward needs to be:

- Organized, as they're often tracking a lot of moving parts.

- Detail-oriented, especially when reviewing data for quality and consistency.
- Analytical, as strong analytical thinking helps a steward understand data patterns and diagnose issues.
- Tenacious, since data problems can be persistent and solving them sometimes takes determination and perseverance.
- Diplomatic, especially when resolving conflicts and negotiating between teams.
- Curious, as great stewards tend to ask good questions and keep digging until they understand what's really going on with the data.

PERSONAL TRAITS

Organized	Detail Oriented	Analytical	Tenacious	Diplomatic	Curious

LEADERSHIP QUALITIES

Communicator	Collaborator	Team Builder	Relationship Builder	Consensus Builder
Critical Thinker	Problem Solver	Facilitator	Influencer	Change Agent

Figure 5: Characteristics of a Data Steward.

Beyond those individual traits, data stewards also rely on leadership qualities—regardless of their job title. They need to be strong communicators and collaborators, because most stewardship work happens across teams. Being a team builder and a relationship builder helps them create the trust and cooperation needed to improve data together. Consensus building is a big part of the job, especially when different people have different expectations about the same data. Stewards also need to think critically and act as problem solvers—not just identifying data issues, but figuring out how to fix them. Other important skills include being a facilitator who helps to guide conversations and decisions. They often act as influencers, getting others to adopt standards and follow policies. They may also need to act as a change agent, especially when improving data means shifting behaviors or processes. While tools and techniques are important, it is these personal and leadership characteristics that ultimately make data stewards effective in the long run.

Summary

Stewardship is disciplined care of a resource over time. Applied to data, it means managing the full lifecycle so data stays understandable, accurate, accessible, secure, and used responsibly. The four ideas that anchor the work are simple and durable: sustainability, conservation, protection, and advocacy. At a high level, these are the things that a data steward actually does:

- connect people, policy, and practice
- coordinate across owners, creators, consumers, architects, and IT
- take hands-on action to improve quality and trust.

Stewardship is viewed through multiple lenses: enterprise, domain (subject/object), business unit, process, and project/system. It is carried out by people with varied backgrounds who share several key traits: being organized, analytical, diplomatic, and curious.

Two

Data Stewardship Organizations

Taking data stewardship seriously means thinking carefully about how to organize it. The way you set things up in terms of who is responsible for what, how issues get handled, and how people work together, has a significant impact on whether stewardship feels like a natural part of the business or just another layer of red tape. Unlike purely technical work, stewardship is as much about people and culture as it is about structure. It's about creating the right connections, encouraging collaboration, and making sure accountability is clear without becoming rigid.

In this chapter, we'll look at the different ways organizations approach stewardship, including hierarchical, matrix, and circular organization models. Formal organization structures benefit when complemented by less formal communities of practice, where stewards share knowledge and support one another. We'll also explore how stewards fit into the bigger picture—working with data owners, architects, governors, producers, and consumers. The purpose is not to describe the perfect model. It is to understand the options, develop ideas about how to mix and match them, and shape the stewardship organization that best fits your organization's culture and level of data maturity.

Hierarchical Organization

So, let's look at how data stewardship can be structured as an organization, starting with the familiar and traditional hierarchy. A hierarchical organizational structure is built on a clear chain of command, with well-defined roles and reporting lines.

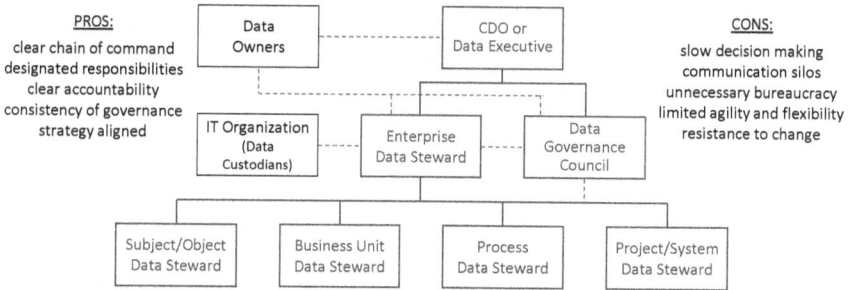

PROS:
clear chain of command
designated responsibilities
clear accountability
consistency of governance
strategy aligned

CONS:
slow decision making
communication silos
unnecessary bureaucracy
limited agility and flexibility
resistance to change

Data Owners — CDO or Data Executive

IT Organization (Data Custodians) — Enterprise Data Steward — Data Governance Council

Subject/Object Data Steward | Business Unit Data Steward | Process Data Steward | Project/System Data Steward

Figure 6: Hierarchical Data Stewardship Organization.

At the top, you usually have a chief data officer or other data executive, setting strategy and policy direction. The enterprise data steward sits just below, responsible for coordinating stewardship activities across the organization. Supporting the enterprise steward, you'll often find data owners, typically senior leaders in business areas, and also IT people who act as data custodians. The data governance council also plays a role, helping guide decisions and align priorities. Below that, you have the different types of stewards—subject, business unit, process, and system—each reporting into the enterprise steward or into their respective business functions, depending on the setup. One of the strengths of this model is clarity. Everyone knows who is responsible for what and how decisions get made. There's consistency across teams, which helps when you're rolling out policies or managing compliance. But it's not without trade-offs. Hierarchical structures can slow things down—especially when approval chains get long. They can also create silos, where teams focus more on their own priorities than on collaboration. In some organizations, the structure can become rigid, making it hard to adapt or respond quickly when data needs change. This model works well in organizations with a strong governance culture and clear lines of accountability. However, it may not be the best fit for highly dynamic or decentralized environments, where flexibility and speed are paramount.

Matrix Organization

The matrix model takes a very different approach from the traditional hierarchy. Instead of a clear chain of command, the matrix emphasizes cross-functional collaboration. In this model, data stewards often report into one group, but work closely with multiple stakeholder groups to coordinate their efforts.

PROS:
cross-functional collaboration
consensus decisions
flexibility and responsiveness
broad SME participation
increased innovation

CONS:
complex reporting relationships
potential role ambiguity
decision-making complexity
conflicting priorities
resource utilization conflicts

CDO or Data Executive

Data Governance Council

Enterprise Data Steward

✔ Reporting Relationship
✔ Stakeholder Relationship

	Subject/Object Data Steward	Business Unit Data Steward	Process Data Steward	Project/System Data Steward
Functional Executives	✓	✔	✓	✓
Process Owners	✓	✓	✔	✓
Data Owners	✔	✓	✓	✓
IT Organization (Data Custodians)	✓	✓	✓	✔

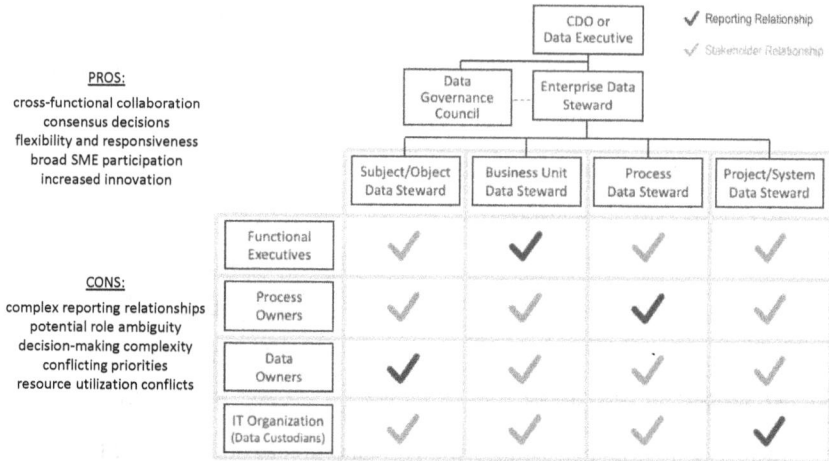

Figure 7: Matrix Data Stewardship Organization.

You can see in the chart that each steward has a primary reporting line, marked in red, and several stakeholder relationships, shown in gray. For example, a business unit data steward might report to a functional executive, but also coordinate with data owners, process owners, and the IT team. The benefit of this structure is flexibility. It gives stewards access to a wide network of subject matter experts and decision-makers, which helps with consensus-building and drives broad participation. That makes the matrix a good fit for responsiveness, adaptability, and innovation. But the matrix can be difficult to manage. It can introduce complex reporting lines, unclear responsibilities, and competing priorities. Decision-making can slow down when multiple groups need to weigh in.

When people are accountable to more than one leader, resource conflicts and misalignment are common challenges. The key to making the matrix work is clarity: clear expectations, well-defined roles, and strong communication. When that's in place, the matrix model creates a space where data stewards can collaborate effectively across boundaries and help the organization move faster and smarter with its data.

Circular Organization

The circular model takes a radically different approach to organizing data stewardship—one that's less about reporting structures and more about connections. Instead of putting people on levels, this model places them in layers. Leadership—usually the chief data officer and enterprise data steward—sit at the center. Around them, you'll find the other data stewards, and beyond that, in the outer ring, are the key stakeholder groups: business executives, process owners, data owners, and IT.

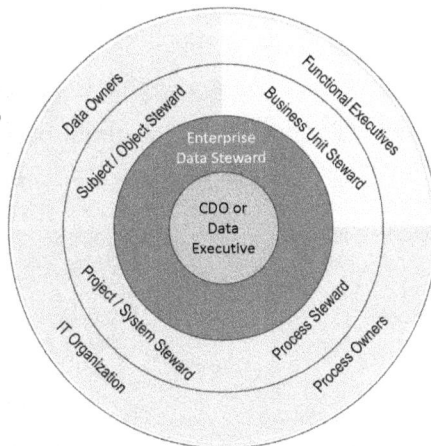

PROS:
enhanced collaboration
agility and flexibility
empowerment and ownership
increased innovation
reduced bureaucracy

CONS:
lack of clear accountability
decision-making bottlenecks
confusion about roles
difficulty scaling
coordination difficulties

Data Owners
Subject / Object Steward
Functional Executives
Business Unit Steward
Enterprise Data Steward
CDO or Data Executive
Project / System Steward
IT Organization
Process Steward
Process Owners

Figure 8: Circular Data Stewardship Organization.

In this model, authority doesn't flow top-down. Decisions and ideas often flow from the outside in, with stakeholders shaping what stewards focus on. The goal is collaboration, not control. Everyone contributes and the structure supports self-managing teams that work together toward shared goals. It's a flexible, lightweight structure. That makes it a good fit for small organizations or teams just starting to formalize their stewardship efforts. Over time, as the program grows, it's often possible to evolve this model into a matrix structure without disrupting too much. The circular approach encourages agility, innovation, and a sense of shared ownership. It reduces bureaucracy and keeps the focus on problem-solving rather than reporting lines. But it's not without challenges.

Without clearly defined roles and reporting relationships, accountability can get fuzzy. Decision-making can stall if there's no agreed-upon process, and as the organization scales, coordination becomes harder unless roles and responsibilities are clarified. This model works best when there's a strong culture of trust and when people are willing to collaborate without needing strict lines of authority. It's all about balance—giving people the space to lead from where they are, while keeping stewardship aligned and effective.

Data Stewardship Communities

So far, we've looked at formal structures for organizing data stewardship—hierarchical, matrix, and circular models. But structure isn't everything. In many organizations, what really makes stewardship effective is the sense of community.

> *A data stewardship community brings people together—not just based on reporting lines or roles, but around a shared purpose: to improve the way the organization manages, understands, and uses data.*

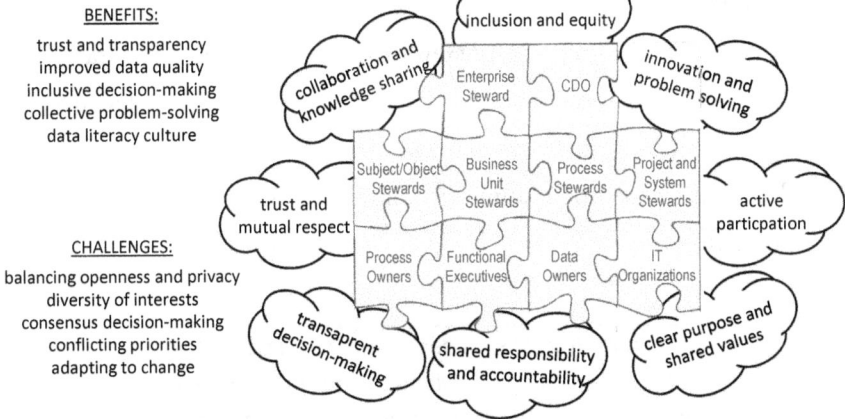

Figure 9: Data Stewardship Community of Practice.

Think of it as a community of practice. It includes stewards of all types, but also data owners, IT professionals, business leaders, and subject matter experts. Everyone plays a part. Everyone contributes insight. Everyone shares responsibility. This puzzle diagram illustrates how everything fits together. The pieces represent different stakeholders. When they connect, they create something bigger than any one role or function. Communities like this offer some real advantages:

- They build trust and transparency
- They support collaborative decision-making and problem-solving
- They improve data quality
- They help create a stronger data literacy culture.

Stewards benefit from working together across boundaries. They share knowledge, solve problems collectively, and help each other build the skills and habits that good data governance depends on. That said, community-based stewardship isn't always easy. It takes active participation and a shared commitment to balance openness with privacy, to manage diverse interests, and to make decisions even when opinions differ. But when it works, it's powerful.

> *Especially in complex or decentralized organizations, a strong stewardship community can accomplish what a formal structure alone can't: connect people, encourage accountability, and build alignment from the inside out.*

Collaborative Data Stewardship: Data Stewards as a Team

One of the most important concepts in modern data stewardship is connecting individual roles to form collaborative teams. While each type of steward—subject, business unit, process, and system—has its own responsibilities, they're most effective when they work together as a team with shared goals and mutual support. The enterprise data steward often plays a central role in that team. They help foster collaboration, mentor individual stewards, and lead initiatives that require coordinated effort across functions. They're also responsible for tracking performance and advocating best practices across the group. Alignment is the key to effective teamwork. This means having a shared purpose, a common governance framework, and consistent methods for measuring success. Frequent communication, shared problem-solving, and an open culture are all essential. Building this kind of team doesn't just happen; it takes intentional effort that requires:

- Visible sponsorship from leadership
- A clear vision and purpose everyone can rally around
- A collaborative culture where participation is encouraged
- Ongoing training and skills development
- Recognition—clear roles and defined expectations
- Incentives for doing stewardship well.

A strong stewardship team isn't just a collection of good individual contributors. It's a group that works together to raise the overall standard of how the organization manages and uses its data.

Data Stewards and Data Owners

Data Owners are individuals responsible for management, oversight, and decision-making for a specific set of data. The data owner has authority and accountability for data quality, security, accessibility, and usage. Owners are typically directors and senior business managers with knowledge of where the data is created and used, as well as an understanding of the legal and regulatory constraints related to the data.

Data stewards and data owners collaborate to ensure that data is not only effectively managed but also aligned with organizational goals and regulatory requirements. Data owners are accountable for the overall quality, accessibility, and usage of data within their domain. They define the business rules, policies, and priorities for data management, ensuring that data supports strategic decision-making.

Data owners are typically responsible for the lifecycle of data within their domain, overseeing data acquisition, storage, and consumption. Stewards, on the other hand, work at a tactical level, ensuring that data is properly maintained and aligned with the organization's needs on a day-to-day basis. They focus on data quality, consistency, and accessibility, ensuring that data adheres to the governance policies set by the data owners. Stewards also ensure that the data remains accurate, reliable, and ready for use.

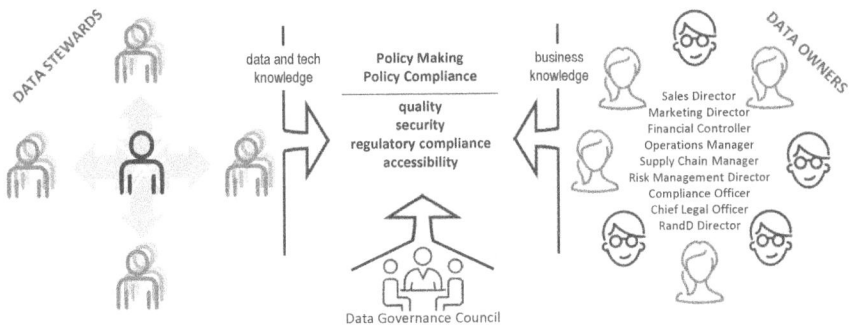

Figure 10: Data Stewards and Data Owners.

The collaboration between stewards and data owners bridges the strategic with the operational. Data owners help stewards understand the broader business goals, regulatory frameworks, and priorities. Data stewards ensure that the operational aspects of data management, such as quality control, data lineage, and usability, are in line with these business goals. Together, owners and stewards focus on areas such as data quality and consistency across business units, alignment with business rules, regulatory compliance, risk management, secure access to sensitive data, and the continuous improvement of data management processes.

> *Data owners often lead in defining data policies and objectives. Stewards work to translate these high-level strategies into everyday practices, ensuring that data is accurate, well-governed, and valuable to the business.*

This partnership ensures that governance policies are not only in place but also adhered to, while maintaining data usability, security, and alignment with the organization's strategic objectives.

Data Stewards and Data Architects

Data Architects design the organization and structure for data storage, data systems, and data infrastructure. Architects ensure that data is collected, stored, integrated, accessed, and utilized efficiently and securely. They prescribe guiding principles, design patterns, and reusable processes that are put into practice by data engineers and data management systems developers. Architectural support of data policies and data governance support of architectural principles work together to ensure effective data management.

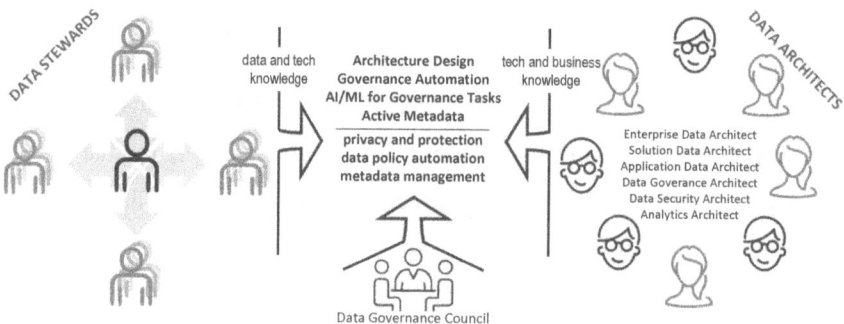

DATA STEWARDS

data and tech knowledge

Architecture Design
Governance Automation
AI/ML for Governance Tasks
Active Metadata

tech and business knowledge

DATA ARCHITECTS

privacy and protection
data policy automation
metadata management

Enterprise Data Architect
Solution Data Architect
Application Data Architect
Data Goverance Architect
Data Security Architect
Analytics Architect

Data Governance Council

Figure 11: Data Stewards and Data Architects.

Data stewards and data architects work closely together to connect policy with practice and design with execution.

Data architects define how data is organized and structured. They design blueprints for data platforms, laying out how data should be stored, integrated, accessed, and protected. They also prescribe the principles, patterns, and models that guide developers, engineers, and platform teams as they implement solutions. Stewards, meanwhile, work at the operational level. They focus on how data actually behaves in the organization, including how it's used, where issues occur, and what needs to be done to keep it accurate, consistent, and usable.

The collaboration between stewards and architects supports both strategy and execution. Stewards help architects ground their designs in real-world use. Architects help stewards scale their practices with tools, models, and automation. Together, they address areas like metadata management, privacy and protection, policy implementation and automation, and governance capabilities powered by active metadata and AI.

Architects often lead the design of technical capabilities. Stewards provide the context needed to ensure those capabilities are aligned with actual data usage, regulatory needs, and governance goals. This partnership establishes a robust connection between governance frameworks and the technical systems that support them, enabling stewardship to be more effective, consistent, and scalable across the organization.

Data Stewards and Data Governors

Data Governors are the individuals responsible for the oversight of policies, standards, principles, and practices to ensure that data is appropriately managed across the enterprise. They are responsible for developing the data management strategy and the policies necessary to implement it as day-to-day practices. Data governance is typically organized as a Data Governance Council that collectively represents the business, technical, architectural, legal, and compliance perspectives of data management.

Data stewards and data governors collaborate to integrate policy with practice. Data governors are responsible for setting direction—defining the principles, policies, and standards that shape how data is managed across the organization. Their focus is on strategy, oversight, and ensuring that data practices align with legal, ethical, and business requirements.

Figure 12: Data Stewards and Data Governors.

Governors are typically organized as a Data Governance Council. This council brings together leaders from across the business—

people with responsibility for risk, compliance, technology, architecture, and operations. Their goal is to take a broad, enterprise-wide view of data and how it should be governed. Stewards are focused on implementation. They put the policies into action through day-to-day data management practices—ensuring quality, enforcing rules, and helping others follow data standards. Data governor and data steward collaboration is essential for success of both data governance and data stewardship.

Governors set the "what"—what the policies are and what the expectations look like. Stewards focus on the "how"—how to make those expectations real in systems, processes, and teams.

Stewards bring data and technology insight into governance discussions. They understand what's possible, where challenges lie, and where exceptions might be needed. Governors contribute business, legal, and strategic perspectives—ensuring that data practices support the organization's broader goals and obligations. This interaction and collaboration help to shape policies that are both sound and practical.

Together, stewards and governors define how the organization approaches:

- Data privacy and protection
- Legal and regulatory compliance
- Quality, retention, and risk

- Metadata management
- Data integration and interoperability
- Business impact and data value.

When the relationship is strong, governance becomes more than just oversight. It becomes a shared commitment to using data responsibly, effectively, and with clear accountability.

Data Stewards and Data Producers

Data Producers are the individuals, teams, systems, and devices that generate, collect, and capture data through business operations, interactions, and automated processes. Data producers include people, business functions, software systems, machines, IoT devices, and external sources. Data production must be attentive to the quality of data generated or collected, as well as to compliance with legal and regulatory requirements when handling and managing data.

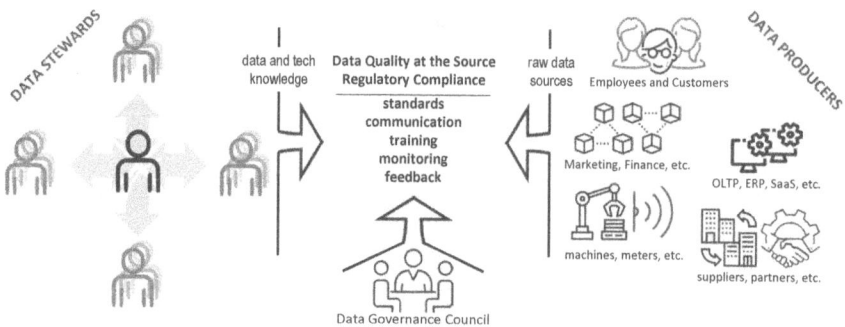

Figure 13: Data Stewards and Data Producers.

The data producer plays a critical role in data quality. Everything downstream depends on how data is initially created. Data producers include a wide range of sources: employees entering data, customers filling out forms, business systems capturing transactions, machines and IoT devices sending readings, and even third-party partners and platforms. If it generates or collects data, it's part of data production.

Data stewards work with producers to make sure that data is created correctly from the start. This is sometimes called "data quality at the source." The goal is to prevent issues before they spread by setting clear standards, training users, monitoring for problems, and giving feedback when things go off track. Steward and producer collaboration is about more than simply correcting errors. It's about preventing errors. More importantly, it's about helping data producers understand their impact. The data that they enter, collect, and automate feeds critical processes like analysis, decision-making, compliance, and customer service.

Stewards bring the data quality lens—defining what "good data" looks like and how to measure it. Producers bring the business and system knowledge—they understand how the data is generated and what constraints they're working within.

Together, they work to improve:

- Input validation
- Process controls

- User interface design
- Feedback loops that help producers improve data over time.

When stewards and producers collaborate well, the entire data lifecycle benefits. Quality improves, rework decreases, and the organization can trust the data it relies on—starting at the source.

Data Stewards and Data Consumers

Data consumers are the people, systems, and processes that rely on data to get things done.

They include business users who run reports, make decisions, and manage operations—and technical users like data engineers and data scientists, who prepare, transform, and analyze data for more advanced use.

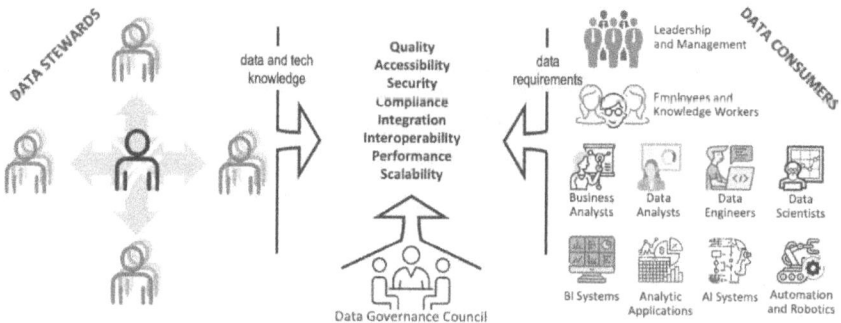

Figure 14: Data Stewards and Data Consumers.

Data stewards work with consumers to make sure that the data they use is trustworthy, accessible, and well understood. Consumers depend on stewards to help ensure data meets key expectations for:

- Quality and accessibility
- Security and compliance
- Integration and interoperability
- Performance and scalability.

At the same time, data consumers help stewards by clarifying their data requirements: what data they need, how they use it, and the challenges they face when it doesn't meet expectations.

This feedback loop is critical. Stewards can't manage data in a vacuum—they need to know how it's being used so they can prioritize the right issues, support data literacy, and improve the overall data experience. This collaboration often includes:

- Identifying critical data elements
- Resolving usability and quality issues
- Aligning metadata with business meaning
- Enabling self-service data access in a responsible way.

When stewards and consumers work together, everyone benefits. Consumers gain confidence in the data they're using, stewards know where to focus their efforts, and the organization builds a strong foundation for data-driven processes and decisions.

Data Stewards and Data Managers

Data managers are the people who make sure the day-to-day work of managing data actually happens. They handle the technical side of things—storage, integration, infrastructure, metadata, security, and everything else needed to keep data flowing and protected.

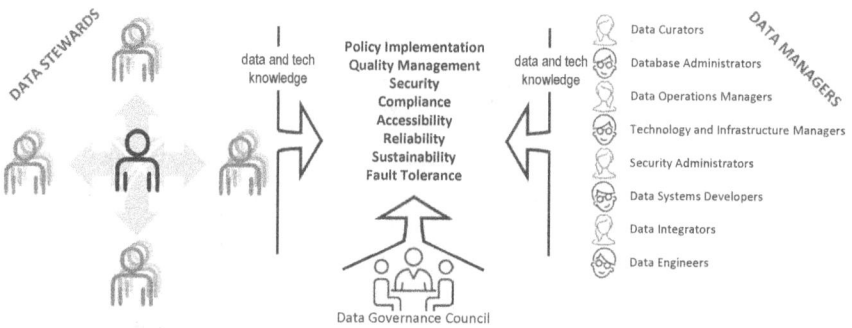

Figure 15: Data Stewards and Data Managers.

Stewards and managers often work side by side. While stewards focus on policy, meaning, and business rules, data managers focus on execution. A few examples of where they collaborate:

- Implementing data policies and standards
- Managing metadata to make data easier to find and use
- Ensuring quality, accessibility, and security
- Supporting disaster recovery, retention, and lifecycle practices.

Data managers serve as the custodians of data—responsible for the infrastructure and tooling that enable policy compliance and reliable operations. Stewards help make sure those systems and tools are aligned with business needs, regulations and governance goals.

> *When the relationship works well, stewards translate intent into clear guidance—and data managers translate that guidance into action. It's a partnership that keeps the entire data ecosystem running smoothly and responsibly.*

Stewardship versus Ownership

Data ownership and data stewardship serve distinct purposes but must work in tandem. Data ownership is strategic. Owners focus on long-term goals, policies, and priorities. They define what needs to be done and why. Ownership entails leadership, accountability, and decision-making authority over data domains. Data stewardship is tactical and operational. At the tactical level, stewards manage policy implementation—deciding when, where, and how data policies are applied. At the operational level, they apply those policies in day-to-day activities. Stewards ensure policy compliance, resolve data issues, and promote good data practices.

> *Ownership sets the direction.*
> *Stewardship plans and guides the journey.*

Effective collaboration between the two ensures that strategy isn't just documented—it's enacted. Owners rely on stewards to interpret and apply their decisions. Stewards rely on owners for clear, actionable guidance. Together, they form a complete governance system—from vision to execution.

Stewardship and Ownership Synergies

Understanding the distinct roles of data owners and data stewards, we can now examine how they collaborate to achieve data governance objectives. This table shows a side-by-side comparison—data governance goals in the first column, followed by the specific roles of owners and stewards for each goal.

You'll notice that data owners are primarily responsible for setting direction—things like defining strategy, setting policy, and providing leadership. Data stewards, on the other hand, bring that direction to life. They translate strategy into tactics, foster compliance, manage operational processes, and carry out the day-to-day activities that make governance work.

Some items—like compliance or access controls—are clearly joint responsibilities. Others show a handoff, where the owner sets policy and the steward ensures it's followed. This kind of clarity is what allows data governance to scale and function effectively across an organization. When ownership and stewardship are aligned, governance goals become achievable.

Data Governance Goal	Owner Role	Steward Role
Sustainability: Endure over the long term	Data management strategy	From strategy to tactics
Conservation: Prevent depletion and loss	Data conservation policies	Foster policy compliance
Protection: Safeguard from harm	Data protection policies	Foster policy compliance
Advocacy: Active and visible support	Vocal and visible sponsorship	Promote best practices
Quality: Suitability to purpose	Establish DQ standards	DQ assessments and projects
Privacy: Personal data controls	Data privacy policies	Foster policy compliance
Security: Defense against intrusion and loss	Data security policies	Foster policy compliance
Access Controls: Permissions and privileges	Data access policies	Foster policy compliance
Compliance: Adherence to policy	Incentives and penalties	Coaching and monitoring
Lifecycle Mgmt: End-to-end controls	Retention and disposal policies	Oversight and coaching
Metadata Mgmt: Data knowledge handling	Metadata standards	Oversight and data cataloging
Integration: Data cohesion and connectivity	Integration goals and standards	Integration practices and projects
Data Ethics: Honest and appropriate data use	Culture and leadership	Advocacy and communication

Table 1: Stewardship and Ownership Synergies.

Who are Data Owners?

Data owners are accountable for the data they oversee. They make decisions about how that data is used, shared, secured, and governed. Ownership includes responsibility for quality, access, protection, and policy compliance. It's a role typically held by business leaders—directors and senior managers—who understand the operational importance of the data and the risks tied to mismanagement. But what makes someone a good data owner? The answer lies in these ten characteristics of effective data ownership:

- **Strategic**: Solid understanding of how data fits into their organization's goals.
- **Data Informed**: Prioritize the use of data to inform decision-making.
- **Data Literate**: Ability to communicate, collaborate, and innovate using data
- **Governance Literate**: Understand governance goals, principles, and practices.
- **Business Literate**: Solid understanding of business concepts and industry practices.
- **Collaborator**: Routinely works with others to achieve common goals.
- **Compliance Aware**: Mindful of legal, regulatory, and contractual constraints.
- **Risk Aware**: Recognizes data risks and works to mitigate them.
- **Active Leadership**: Engaged, visible, and leading by example.
- **Culture Builder**: Actively works to shape and strengthen data culture.

No single person will excel in all ten, and that's okay. What's important is understanding each owner's strengths—and where they might need support or development. Some traits, such as being strategic and data-informed, involve aligning data with business priorities. Others, like governance literacy and compliance awareness, reflect a working knowledge of policies, standards, and regulatory constraints. You'll also see characteristics like collaborator, active leadership, and culture builder. These emphasize that data ownership isn't just about data and technology—it's also about working with people, building trust, and helping to shape a data-savvy culture.

Three characteristics are essential: data literacy, governance literacy, and business literacy. Every data owner should strive to be capable in these areas, as they form the foundation for effective decision-making and communication in the ownership role.

Why Data Ownership Matters

Data ownership matters both to the culture of your data environment and the management of your data assets. Ownership creates clarity. It establishes accountability, aligns policies with business leadership, and enables sound, secure, and ethical data practices. These impacts show up in two main areas: data culture and data management. A strong data culture depends on clearly defined ownership. Authority means that decision-making power is clearly designated. There's no ambiguity about who can make the call.

- **Accountability** ensures someone is answerable for data outcomes—good or bad. This is vital for trust and results.
- **Policies** are stronger when shaped by business leaders. Ownership connects data policy to business goals.
- **Transparency** grows when roles are visible and clear. People are more likely to engage with governance when it's open and honest.
- **Participation** matters. Ownership promotes inclusive governance—encouraging collaboration and building buy-in.
- **Structure** keeps things organized. A defined ownership framework reduces silos, overlap, and redundancy.

Together, these characteristics create a culture where data is managed with purpose—and with people at the center. From access control to ethics, data ownership plays a central role in everyday data management.

- **Access Controls** are the owner's responsibility. They define who can see and use data—and who cannot.
- **Security and Privacy** require active ownership. Oversight ensures safeguards are in place and risk is minimized.

- **Data Quality Management** works best under owner direction. Owners frame the goals—stewards carry them out.
- **Legal and Compliance** oversight isn't optional. Ownership facilitates the interpretation and application of external regulations and internal policies.
- **Data Ethics** is a growing concern. Owners help prevent misuse and reinforce responsible data behavior.

Stewardship depends on ownership. Data stewards work under the guidance and authority of data owners. Ownership turns governance from theory into active data management practices. It ensures that the strategy is supported with structure, clarity, and accountability.

Summary

Effective stewardship is a design choice. Choose a structure (or hybrid) that makes accountability explicit, creates easy paths for collaboration, and scales with your culture and maturity. Use communities of practice to keep knowledge moving. Anchor the model in real partnerships—owners for direction, stewards for execution, architects for design, governors for oversight, and producers and consumers for outcomes. When roles are clear and connections are strong, stewardship stops being an add-on and becomes the way the organization works with data.

THREE

Data Steward
Roles and Responsibilities

Data stewardship encompasses a dynamic set of roles that stewards must shift between as circumstances demand. Some days they lead, setting direction and influencing culture. On other days, they manage project details, facilitate discussions between stakeholders, or troubleshoot persistent data issues. Often, they coach others to build literacy and confidence with data. These roles overlap and intersect, and effective stewardship depends on the ability to recognize what the situation requires and step into that role with purpose.

This chapter explores the various roles of data stewardship—leader, manager, facilitator, problem solver, and coach—and demonstrates how these roles translate into tangible responsibilities. We have already described steward as a role—not a position or job title. In this context, "roles" refers to the different modes of responsibility and activity within the broader function of being a steward—a roles-within-a-role concept. The chapter examines how stewards contribute to strategy and execution, how they build trust through policy and protection, and how they nurture the skills and culture needed for responsible data use. Taken together, these roles and responsibilities illustrate why stewardship involves so much more than simply enforcing compliance.

> *Effective data stewardship enables collaboration, fosters connections, engages stakeholders, and ensures that data supports the organization's goals and needs.*

Data Steward Roles

Data stewards assume various roles, depending on the circumstances and needs that can change from day to day. At times, stewards are leaders, shaping direction and inspiring change. At other times, they serve as managers guiding projects and activities to perform data management and data governance tasks. Stewards are often called to be facilitators, guiding conversations, consensus, and collaboration among various data stakeholders. When issues arise, they become problem solvers, diagnosing causes and guiding the path to resolution. With goals to develop data literacy and build capabilities, they serve as coaches, helping others to understand policies, practices, and the "why" behind them. Every steward fills multiple roles when and as they are needed. No steward plays only one of these parts. Strong stewardship requires flexibility—the ability to move between roles as needed and to simultaneously fill multiple roles.

Data Stewards as Leaders

Stewardship is a leadership role. I don't mean leadership in the hierarchical sense, but in the sense of taking initiative, guiding action, and influencing culture. Sometimes it is project leadership—guiding initiatives to improve quality, implement a data catalog, and similar efforts. Sometimes, it's thought leadership—shaping standards, definitions, and practices that ripple across the organization. They may also step into cultural leadership as advocates for responsible data use, data ethics, and data literacy—influential leadership that shapes how people think about and interact with data. Some of the key areas where stewards may provide leadership include:

- **Data Quality**: Accuracy, completeness, consistency, objectivity, and reliability of data.

- **Data Cataloging**: Metadata collection, catalog training, and adoption.

- **Metadata Management**: Standards, processes and practices, and metadata quality.

- **Data Policy Implementation**: Standards, guidelines, training and awareness, and issue resolution.

- **Compliance and Auditing**. Compliance observation, monitoring, and review.

- **Data Classification and Protection**. Sensitivity classification of data and data protection policies.

- **Data Accessibility and Availability**. Access control policies, retention, and availability SLAs.

- **Data Literacy**: Data literacy goals and plans, and data literacy training.

- **Data Ethics and Responsible Use**. Ethics guidelines and training, and data use transparency.

- **Data Collaboration**. Data sharing policies and fostering cross-functional collaboration.

Remember that leadership in each of these areas may be any combination of project leadership, thought leadership, and cultural leadership.

Data Stewards as Managers

Data stewardship includes a strong management component. Stewards are responsible for setting goals, planning how to achieve them, tracking progress, and evaluating outcomes. This work plays out in the day-to-day management of data practices across the organization. The practical scope of stewardship management includes familiar domains such as quality, governance, privacy, metadata, and lifecycle management—but with an emphasis on execution. It's not just about defining standards; it's about putting them into practice. That includes reducing vulnerabilities, managing retention and disposal, aligning projects to priorities, and fostering trust with data stakeholders.

Data Stewards as Facilitators

Data stewards often take on a facilitation role—not by controlling conversations, but by guiding them. They help groups set shared ground rules, ask thoughtful questions, and actively listen to different points of view. They foster participation by creating safe environments where diverse ideas are welcome and feedback is encouraged. The role as facilitator is to establish mutual respect, promote inclusiveness, and encourage clear and direct communication. They bring structure to meetings, clarify goals and roles, and help groups build consensus. Good facilitators know how to manage time, navigate conflict, and keep discussions on track without shutting anyone down. They clarify objectives, acknowledge differences, and help people find common ground. Reflection and learning also matter. Stewards guide teams to recognize what's working, what needs attention, and how to grow from experience. Facilitation work builds trust, strengthens collaboration, and supports shared commitments to data governance goals.

Data Stewards as Problem Solvers

Frequently, the most pressing work of data stewards is problem-solving. They step in when issues arise with data quality, data definitions, naming standards, access controls, and integration approaches. Their role is to frame the problem clearly, analyze the causes, and apply appropriate methods to resolve and prevent recurrence.

Solving data problems requires more than technical skills. Stewards must understand business meaning, policy context, and usage expectations. For example, if data names are confusing or inconsistent, they work to standardize naming conventions. If definitions vary across systems, they clarify and document terms to eliminate ambiguity. They apply design thinking to create coherent and integrity-driven data structures. They define quality measures, set targets, and monitor results to ensure data serves its intended purpose.

Stewards also troubleshoot integration challenges—tracing how data moves and transforms across systems. They identify metadata gaps, uncover access issues, and resolve conflicts in database or system management. When they solve problems, they don't just fix what's broken. They build preventive practices that improve trust, transparency, and long-term sustainability. As problem solvers, data stewards combine root cause analysis with proactive solutions—contributing to a strong and resilient data environment.

Data Stewards as Coaches

Data stewards are also coaches—guiding others to build knowledge, apply skills, and grow confidence in using data. As coaches, stewards help individuals and teams understand their roles in data governance, data management, data creation and acquisition, data consumption and analysis, data protection and privacy, and responsible data use. They clarify how each person contributes to the broader data ecosystem and why their participation matters.

Data stewards promote data literacy—helping others interpret data, find meaning, and communicate insights. They guide colleagues to recognize good data practices, comply with policies, and respect legal and regulatory requirements.

Stewards coach on a wide range of data skills: how to acquire the right data, prepare and cleanse it, analyze it effectively, and present findings through charts, graphs, dashboards, and data storytelling. They reinforce data ethics—helping others make decisions that are both effective and responsible. In the coaching role, data stewards promote teamwork, adaptability, and accountability. Their influence extends beyond process and policy—they support people and help build a strong data culture of shared understanding and applied skills.

Data Stewardship Responsibilities

Data stewards have a wide range of responsibilities that extend from strategy to tactics and execution. The work is not limited to a single task or discipline. Instead, stewardship requires balancing multiple priorities—setting direction, enabling collaboration, and ensuring that data is managed as an asset throughout its lifecycle.

At a strategic level, stewards contribute as advisors and planners. They help shape policies, align data practices with business goals, and provide guidance on issues like governance, architecture, and quality. On a daily basis, they put strategy into action by overseeing policies, monitoring compliance, managing metadata, and bridging the gaps between business and technology teams and stakeholders. Ultimately, their effectiveness is measured by the outcomes they achieve: building a culture of data-informed decision-making, trusted data, responsible data use, business agility and data-driven innovation.

Taken together, these responsibilities illustrate the multi-dimensional nature of stewardship. Each area—whether quality, literacy, compliance, collaboration, or ethics—demands attention and skill.

Stewardship and Data Strategy

Although we previously positioned data stewardship as tactical and operational, stewards also have data strategy roles and responsibilities. Data stewards play an important part across three levels of strategy work: strategy formation, tactical execution, and strategic outcomes.

At the strategy level, stewards serve as advisors and contributors. Their insight into governance, quality, privacy, lifecycle, and usage helps shape strategic planning that is both sound and practical. They bring real-world data knowledge to planning discussions that focus on architecture, analytics, interoperability, governance, and collaboration as elements of data strategy.

Tactically, stewards are responsible for putting strategy into action. They carry out key tasks: overseeing policy, maintaining data quality, managing metadata, classifying access, and monitoring compliance. They also bridge the gap between business and technical teams and guide both data creators and data users in applying strategy to everyday practices.

DATA STEWARDS HAVE KEY ROLES IN CREATING and EXECUTING DATA STRATEGY

STRATEGY	TACTICS	OUTCOMES
Strategic Planning Advisor/Contributor:	**Day-to-Day Execution of Strategy:**	**Contributor to Achieving Strategic Goals:**
• Governance	• Oversee policies	• Culture of Data-Informed Decisions
• Architecture	• Foster literacy	• Data Quality Awareness
• Quality	• Advocate for best practices	• Operational Efficiency
• Consumption (BI, Analytics, AI/ML)	• Monitor and maintain quality	• Customer Experience and Personalization
• Security and Privacy	• Manage metadata	• Data Security and Compliance Practices
• Culture and Literacy	• Classify data for access	• Data as a Foundation of Innovation
• Integration and Interoperability	• Bridge between business and tech	
• Data Lifecycle	• Manage the data lifecycle	
• Collaboration and Sharing	• Train and guide creators and consumers	
	• Monitor compliance	
	• Monitor security and access	

Figure 16: Stewardship and Data Strategy.

At the outcome level, stewards help organizations achieve the intended results of their data strategy. Their ongoing efforts support data-informed decisions, build awareness of data quality, improve operational efficiency, and strengthen privacy and compliance. Through their work, stewards help position data as a foundation for innovation and competitive advantage.

Strategy, tactics, and outcomes—
data stewards are essential across all three.

Stewardship and Data Literacy

Data stewards foster both individual and organizational data literacy, building the skills and habits needed to understand, use, and question data effectively.

Data steward work includes activities specifically related to literacy. Stewards may be responsible for providing learning resources and creating hands-on opportunities by enabling sandbox environments for experimentation and exploration. They foster literacy by guiding and mentoring individuals and teams—the work of sharing knowledge, building skills, and offering constructive feedback. And importantly, they promote a mindset that values curiosity, awareness, and evidence-based decision-making. These activities build the foundation of data literacy knowledge and skills. Individuals learn to understand data in context, to think critically about what it means, and to question assumptions. They become more skilled in communicating with data, especially through visualization and storytelling. They gain the ability to apply data practically—to solve problems and make informed decisions.

Data literacy also includes understanding the limitations of data—recognizing uncertainty, identifying scope, and challenging assumptions. It includes learning how to use data responsibly, with attention to ethics, legal obligations, and regulatory compliance. In short, stewards help people do more than use data—they help them use it wisely, responsibly, and effectively.

Stewardship and Data Policies

Policy Making: Data stewards have important roles in policy making, policy management, and policy compliance. First, we'll focus on their participation in policymaking. The process begins when stewards or others identify the need for a policy. This may arise from a lack of regulation, inconsistencies in practice, or the need to clarify standards. Next, stewards research and analyze the situation, gathering facts and understanding the potential consequences of policy decisions. They then consult with stakeholders, engaging data owners, subject matter experts, legal advisors, and others to ensure that multiple perspectives are considered.

With input gathered, stewards draft the policy, working to clearly define the purpose, scope, definitions, roles, and responsibilities. The draft then goes through review and feedback. Stewards facilitate stakeholder feedback to assess clarity and practicality, making revisions if needed. Once the policy is refined, stewards help finalize and approve it, often collaborating with governing bodies or councils to obtain formal authorization. The final step in the policy-making process is distribution and communication. Stewards ensure that the policy is well communicated and understood by the people it affects—setting the stage for successful policy management and compliance. Throughout this entire process, stewards collaborate closely with the data governance council.

It's a team effort—grounded in shared responsibility and informed decision-making.

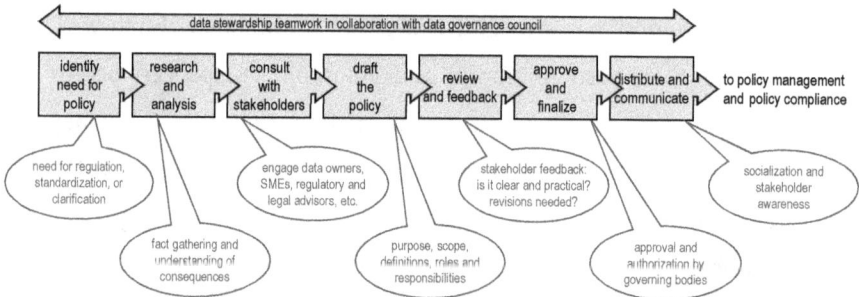

Figure 17: Data Stewardship and Policy Making.

Policy Maintenance: Creating and adopting policies is only the beginning. Policy maintenance is an ongoing responsibility—and one where data stewards play a central role. Stewards routinely review policies to assess their current relevance and effectiveness. This helps identify which policies still serve their intended purpose and which may need updates.

They also monitor changes in laws, regulations, and standards. Data policies must remain compliant and aligned with external requirements, so stewards stay alert to legal and regulatory shifts. Another critical activity is gap analysis. Stewards evaluate how well policies address current needs, determine if there are any coverage gaps, and assess whether policies are clear, complete, and actionable. Seeking feedback is part of this ongoing process. Stewards solicit input from the people who use and follow the policies, capturing practical insights that can inform and guide improvements. Maintaining a change history is equally important. Stewards document each policy update, noting what changed, when it changed, and why. This creates transparency and a valuable audit trail. Finally, stewards manage policy termination. When a policy becomes outdated or redundant, stewards ensure that it's formally retired—and archived when appropriate—as part of the organization's historical record. Data stewards are responsible for six key activities related to policy maintenance:

- **Regular Policy Review**: Routinely and frequently assess the relevance and effectiveness of existing policies.

- **Change Monitoring**: Maintain up-to-date knowledge of laws, regulations, and standards related to policies.

- **Gap Analysis**: Evaluate effectiveness, change impacts, completeness, and clarity of policies.

- **Seeking Feedback**: Solicit and respond to feedback from stakeholders who must adhere to policies.

- **Change History**: Keep records of policy versions and changes, including dates and reasons for changes.

- **Termination of Policies**: Recognition and termination of obsolete policies with archiving as historical records.

Taken together, these activities ensure that data policies remain current, relevant and effective over time. This is one of the ways that data stewardship reinforces policy integrity and supports sustainable governance.

Policy Compliance: The final stage of policy work is ensuring compliance—and data stewards play an active role here as well.

Compliance isn't only about enforcement; it begins with enablement and support. Stewards can help to prevent policy violations by showing people how to comply. They create guides, such as flowcharts, step-by-step instructions, reusable processes, and interactive help. These resources simplify compliance by clearly outlining what to do and how to do it.

Stewards support intervention with guardrails that help prevent accidental violations. Think of intuitive user interfaces, automated alerts, built-in review steps, and embedded policy awareness in workflows. These mechanisms reduce the likelihood of mistakes by guiding people before issues occur.

When necessary, stewards contribute to enforcement. This is the last line of defense—where gates are used to stop violations. These include authentication, access controls, and other technical safeguards that prevent unauthorized actions and access.

Guides help people navigate data policies with confidence and accuracy. Guardrails steer people away from potential missteps. Gates prevent or block actions that violate policy. Together, these three layers—prevention, intervention, and enforcement—create a comprehensive policy compliance framework that data stewards help to implement, maintain, and adapt over time.

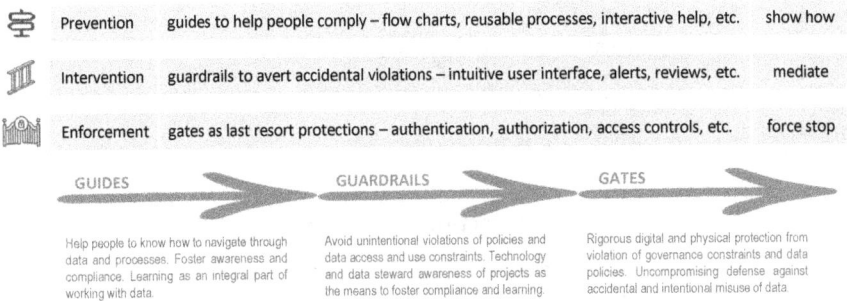

Prevention	guides to help people comply – flow charts, reusable processes, interactive help, etc.	show how
Intervention	guardrails to avert accidental violations – intuitive user interface, alerts, reviews, etc.	mediate
Enforcement	gates as last resort protections – authentication, authorization, access controls, etc.	force stop

GUIDES	GUARDRAILS	GATES
Help people to know how to navigate through data and processes. Foster awareness and compliance. Learning as an integral part of working with data.	Avoid unintentional violations of policies and data access and use constraints. Technology and data steward awareness of projects as the means to foster compliance and learning.	Rigorous digital and physical protection from violation of governance constraints and data policies. Uncompromising defense against accidental and intentional misuse of data.

Figure 18: Data Stewardship and Policy Compliance.

Stewardship and Data Protection

Data protection is essential to earning and keeping stakeholder trust, and to compliance with contractual, legal, and regulatory constraints. And data stewards have a vital role to play. Working in partnership with data owners, IT, security, and data governors, stewards help with translating protection requirements into practical actions. Stewards:

- Help ensure protection policy compliance, applying methods across prevention, intervention, and enforcement to drive adherence.

- Apply sensitive data classification by working with data owners and governance teams, labeling data based on risk level—public, internal, confidential, or restricted.

- Monitor data access, routinely reviewing authorizations to help limit exposure and prevent inappropriate access.

- Ensure secure data disposal when data reaches the end of its lifecycle, coordinating with IT to guarantee that sensitive data is unrecoverable.

- Foster a data protection culture, encouraging all data users to understand their responsibilities and take protective actions seriously.

- Contribute to security incident responses, helping identify risks, mitigate impacts, and support resolution efforts.

- Assist IT teams in validating security methods and solutions, ensuring appropriate tools and safeguards are in place.

- Participate in data protection audits, examining access practices, controls, and compliance with established standards.

- Promote privacy by design and privacy by default—
embedding protection into systems and processes from
the start and making privacy the standard practice, not
an exception.

Stewards don't work alone—they collaborate with data owners,
IT, security teams, developers, governance councils, and business
leaders. Together, they create a strong, safe, and resilient data
environment.

Stewardship and Data Quality

Data stewards take an active role to ensure that data meets defined
quality expectations by:

- Setting quality standards by defining specific criteria and
measurement methods.

- Assessing data to identify defects and determine where
improvement is needed.

- Detecting problems and correcting them directly or
applying data cleansing tools.

- Defining validation rules and making sure data creators
and systems apply those rules at the point of entry.

- Monitoring data quality over time to detect changes and
uncover new issues.

- Analyzing the root causes of problems and taking corrective and preventive actions.

- Leading projects to improve data quality and reduce recurring issues.

- Enriching data by adding trusted external information.

- Managing metadata to clarify meaning, track lineage, and support quality goals.

- Preventing defects before they occur and advocating practices to build quality into systems from the start.

- Working closely with business leaders and governance councils to support quality by design as a standard operating principle.

Stewardship and Metadata Management

Data stewards act as catalysts to strengthen metadata practices and advance metadata maturity across the organization. They work in partnership with data architects, engineers, and the data governance council to guide improvements and support continued adoption of best practices. Stewards work to establish and promote standards for capturing, storing, and using metadata. They advocate for metadata creation and collection as part of everyday data processes and support efforts to embed metadata practices into data workflows.

While they may not directly own infrastructure such as metadata repositories, stewards contribute by participating in efforts to create or enhance a centralized, trusted source of metadata. They encourage practices that improve metadata quality, promoting completeness, accuracy, and validation. To foster interoperability, stewards help align metadata across systems and platforms. They support data tagging practices to improve searchability and to identify sensitive data, even when tagging depends on tools or actions outside of their direct control. Similarly, they influence access control practices by collaborating with others to ensure sensitive metadata is appropriately protected.

Stewards also help evolve data cataloging by encouraging the use of trusted external sources for metadata enrichment and by promoting active catalog adoption among data users. They work with teams to embed automated metadata capture into data processes—advocating for metadata by design.

In all of these activities, data stewards guide progress, champion best practices, and help the organization mature its metadata management capabilities over time.

Summary

Data stewardship is not a single role or responsibility—it is a mix of multiple roles where flexibility, adaptability, and balance are required. Steward is itself a role, but within that role stewards shift among different modes of responsibility and activity. They lead when direction and influence are needed, manage when plans must be executed, facilitate when diverse voices need to be heard, solve problems when challenges arise, and coach to build confidence and capabilities. These roles overlap. They move and shift depending on context and circumstances. The strongest stewards are those who recognize what is required in the moment and step into it effectively.

Beyond the roles, stewardship carries a wide set of responsibilities that reach from daily operations to long-term strategy. Stewards help shape policy, promote literacy, guide compliance, strengthen metadata, and safeguard data quality and protection. They work at both the human and the technical levels, bridging gaps, translating needs, and enabling trust in data. The value extends beyond the activities they perform, reaching to the culture they foster—a culture where data is respected, used responsibly, and positioned as a true organizational asset.

Taken together, these roles and responsibilities show that data stewardship is not just about enforcing rules or maintaining systems. It is about building connections, enabling collaboration, and ensuring that data continues to serve the goals of the business. With stewards guiding both people and processes, organizations are equipped to navigate complexity, reduce risk, and unlock the value of their data.

FOUR

Data Stewardship Knowledge Areas

Data stewardship encompasses a comprehensive body of knowledge that includes concepts and capabilities related to business, data, and people. All stewards need a shared foundation of knowledge, but no single person is expected to be an expert in everything. To manage stewardship knowledge across a team of data stewards, it is important to distinguish between primary knowledge (must-have for a given role) and secondary knowledge that rounds out and enriches individual capabilities. What's primary or secondary varies by steward type (enterprise, subject/object, business unit, process, project/system), but every knowledge area is primary for at least one role.

Knowledge by Type of Steward

Different steward roles emphasize different areas of expertise. An enterprise steward may need a broad view of strategy and compliance, while a project steward might focus on the practical execution of project activities and system-level details. To clarify these distinctions, the following graph organizes knowledge areas by steward type, distinguishing between deep expertise as primary knowledge and general awareness and understanding as secondary knowledge. The comparison illustrates how stewardship knowledge is distributed across roles and why a team approach to stewardship is essential.

It is significant that four particularly important knowledge areas—Data Fundamentals, Data Quality, Communication, and Collaboration are recognized as primary knowledge for all data stewards. This is a baseline set of knowledge that every steward relies upon every day.

Consider the primary versus secondary designations as guidelines that represent the author's experiences and impressions about where depth is expected and where awareness and fundamental knowledge are sufficient. Your organization and your data stewardship leaders may have different needs, experiences, and impressions. Don't hesitate to adapt to best fit your data stewardship program.

Business Knowledge
- Industry Practices
- Business Functions
- Data Strategy
- Regulatory & Compliance

Data Knowledge
- Data Fundamentals
- Data Quality
- Metadata Management
- Data Architecture
- Integration & Interoperability
- Security & Privacy
- Data Creation
- Data Consumptioin

Human and Interpersonal Knowledge
- Communication
- Group Dynamics
- Collaboration
- Change Management
- Policy Compliance
- Coaching

Columns: Enterprise Steward | Subject/Object Steward | Business Unit Steward | Process Steward | Project/System Steward

Legend: primary | secondary

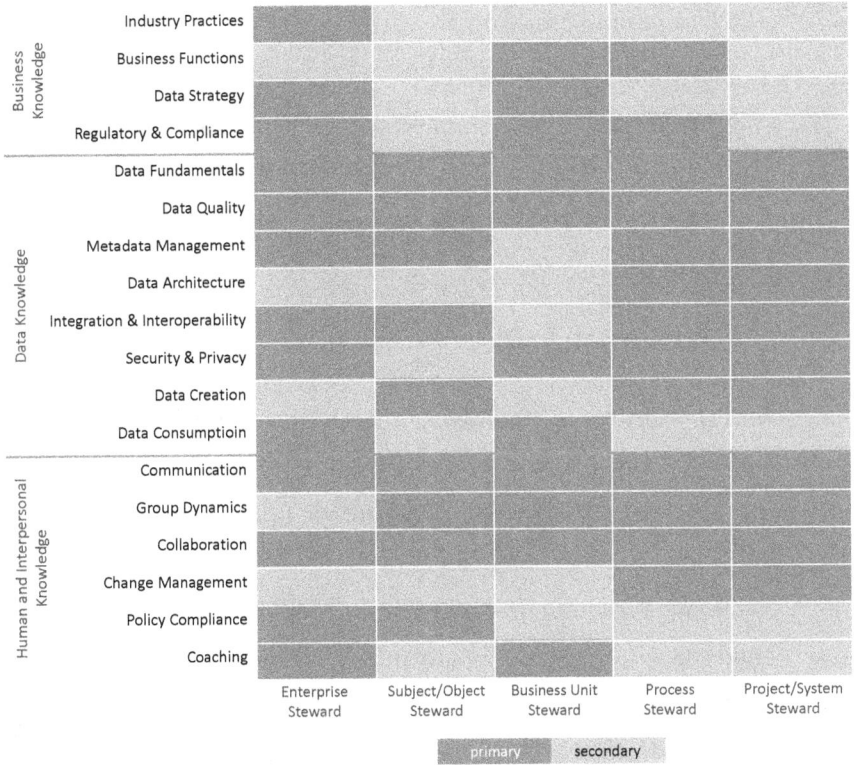

Figure 19: Primary and Secondary Knowledge by Steward Type.

A Deeper Look at the Knowledge Areas

Each knowledge area represents a body of concepts, principles, and topics that stewards need to understand. The following drill-down descriptions are designed to unpack what each area includes—to expand and provide greater detail. They highlight elements of knowledge that give shape and depth to stewardship practices.

The lists of topics for each area are descriptive, not prescriptive. They offer practical insights into what needs to be known and where to focus attention. Stewards, stewardship teams, and leaders can use these lists to identify strengths, recognize gaps, and plan learning and growth activities.

Business Knowledge

Industry Practices Knowledge covers the external context in which an organization operates, including its core functions, market structure, regulations, and norms. For data stewards, this knowledge enables them to anticipate external pressures that shape data requirements, risks, and opportunities. In data management, it guides the alignment of internal practices with industry standards, benchmarks, and compliance expectations. For the business, it ensures data supports competitiveness, regulatory adherence, and responsiveness to trends and disruptions. Topics include:

- Industry structure (value chains, business models, and players)
- Regulatory and standards bodies (sector codes and oversight groups)
- Common industry data patterns (benchmarks and seasonal cycles)
- Industry reference data sources and conventions
- External data providers and market datasets
- Sector-specific risks and compliance requirements

- Emerging trends and disruptions affecting data needs
- Peer practices for reporting and KPIs.

Business Functions Knowledge centers on how data supports the major operational areas of the organization, such as finance, HR, supply chain, and sales. For data stewards, this means recognizing critical data elements, processes, and decision points within each function related to their scope of stewardship responsibilities. In data management, it ensures stewardship focuses on data that directly impacts operational performance and functional integrity. Critical Data Elements (CDEs) are a key part of that focus. They are the most important data fields for business operations, decisions, and compliance. For the business, this knowledge helps to ensure that data stewardship is practical, relevant, and aligned with the drivers of efficiency, compliance, and value creation. Topics include:

- Functional domains (finance, HR, supply chain, operations, sales, etc.)
- Key processes and workflows in each domain
- Function-specific KPIs and decisions
- Critical Data Elements (CDEs) tied to functions
- Functional data issues and their business impact
- Data privacy/security needs by function
- Systems of record and analytic systems used in each domain
- Functional change drivers (regulatory, competitive, and organizational).

Data Strategy Knowledge links stewardship to broader organizational objectives, investments, and outcomes. For data stewards, it provides the ability to prioritize data initiatives, balance value and risk, and connect stewardship to governance and architecture roadmaps. In data management, it creates alignment between tactical stewardship work and strategic direction. For the business, it ensures that data stewardship contributes to measurable goals, responsible data use, and sustained return on data investments. Topics include:

- Business strategy and its data implications
- Critical Data Elements (CDEs) identification and prioritization
- Data value versus risk tradeoffs
- Alignment with data governance and architecture roadmaps
- Data ethics and responsible use considerations
- Investment planning for data initiatives
- Strategic measures of success
- Feedback loops between strategy and operations.

Regulatory and Compliance Knowledge addresses contract, policy, legal, and regulatory regulations, ensuring data is managed lawfully, ethically, and with awareness of regional differences. For data stewards, this knowledge guides decisions about retention, classification, protection, and use of sensitive data. In data management, it embeds compliance requirements into everyday practices, systems, and audits. For the business, it mitigates risk, avoids penalties, and strengthens trust with customers, partners, and regulators. Topics include:

- Key privacy and security regulations (GDPR, CCPA, HIPAA, etc.)
- Contractual data obligations
- Data sovereignty and localization requirements
- Retention and disposal rules
- Sensitive data classification categories
- Auditing requirements (evidence, lineage, and approvals)
- Policy guardrails (guides, guardrails, and gates)
- Monitoring and exception handling processes.

Data Knowledge

Data Fundamentals provide the language, concepts, and structures that underlie all stewardship work. For data stewards, this knowledge creates a foundation to understand definitions, identifiers, relationships, semantics, data dynamics, and data management practices. In data management, it supports consistency, interoperability, and traceability. For the business, it enables clear communication, trusted reporting, and sound decision-making based on a shared understanding of data. Topics include:

- Data types (master, reference, transactional, and analytical)

- Identifiers, keys, and relationships (cardinality and hierarchies)
- Definitions, glossaries, and semantic alignment
- Provenance and lineage basics
- Granularity, precision, and timeliness concepts
- Common sources of bias in data
- Naming conventions and value standards
- Metadata basics related to the meaning and structure of data.

Data Quality Knowledge guides the processes and practices to ensure that data is correct in content, structurally sound, usable for intended purposes, and free from bias. For data stewards, this knowledge supports activities to measure, monitor, and improve quality. In data management, it fosters practices to correct defects, prevent defects, and address root causes. For the business, it reduces the cost of errors, improves operational efficiency, and enhances confidence in data-driven decisions. Topics include:

- Dimensions of quality (correctness, integrity, usability, and objectivity)
- Quality measurement methods and thresholds
- Defect detection versus prevention versus correction
- Root cause analysis for quality issues
- Quality costs and business impact
- Quality by design practices
- Data profiling and monitoring techniques
- Quality indicators and scorecards.

Metadata Management Knowledge supports the understanding of data through documentation, cataloging, classification, and adherence to standards. For data stewards, it means using metadata to capture meaning, lineage, ownership, and context. In data management, it provides transparency into how data is structured, transformed, and used. For the business, it builds confidence in data assets, supports compliance, and improves the discoverability and usability of data. Topics include:

- Business metadata (definitions, glossaries, and ownership)
- Technical metadata (schemas, columns, and formats)
- Operational metadata (processes, lineage, and run logs)
- Quality metadata (defects, thresholds, and health indicators)
- Lineage metadata (flows, transformations, and dependencies)
- Semantic metadata (taxonomies, ontologies, and vocabularies)
- Metadata lifecycle (capture, curate, govern, maintain, and retire)
- Metadata tools (catalogs, glossaries, and lineage repositories).

Data Architecture Knowledge supports understanding of how data is structured, processed, integrated, protected, and managed across systems. For data stewards, it creates awareness of the environments, models, and patterns that shape data availability and quality. In data management, it aligns stewardship with standards for schema design, lifecycle transitions, and resiliency. For the business, it shapes how data is managed to achieve scalability, interoperability, and reliability for both operations and analytics. Topics include:

- Architectural patterns (warehouse, lake, lakehouse, mesh, fabric, etc.)
- Operational versus analytical data
- Architectural challenges (data silos, disparity, etc.)
- Data models (relational, dimensional, and semantic)
- Data flows (logical, physical, and lineage)
- Schema design concepts
- Lifecycle activities (create, acquire, ingest, transform, archive, purge, etc.)
- Architectural standards and patterns
- Observability and resiliency design principles.

Integration and Interoperability Knowledge supports understanding of processes and techniques that enable data to move across systems while retaining meaning. For data stewards, it means understanding schema-level integration and semantic-level interoperability, along with methods such as ETL, virtualization, and APIs. In data management, it supports reliable data pipelines, data equivalence, and semantic reconciliation. For the business, it improves agility, reduces redundancy, and makes it possible to connect insights across domains in real time. Topics include:

- Integration versus interoperability

- Methods (ETL/ELT, virtualization, streaming, etc.)
- Data mapping and transformation concepts
- Shared vocabularies, taxonomies, and ontologies
- API standards and interface contracts
- Reference data alignment (identifiers and codes)
- Pipeline reliability and monitoring
- Semantic equivalence and reconciliation.

Security and Privacy Knowledge underlies processes and practices to ensure that sensitive and regulated data is protected throughout its lifecycle. For data stewards, it involves applying classification schemes, access controls, and privacy principles to everyday stewardship activities. In data management, it embeds safeguards such as encryption, masking, and monitoring into practices and systems. For the business, it reduces exposure to breaches, builds trust, and supports legal and ethical use of data. Topics include:

- Data classification levels (public, internal, confidential, and restricted)
- Access control models (role-based and attribute-based controls, and least privilege access rights)
- Privacy-by-design and privacy-by-default principles
- Data lifecycle handling (collection, retention, and disposal)
- Encryption, masking, and tokenization
- Incident response and remediation processes
- Consent management and lawful basis for processing
- Audit and monitoring practices.

Data Creation Knowledge emphasizes getting data right at the source—ensuring accuracy, validity, context, and consistency of meaning at the point of origin. For data stewards, this means defining standards for values and quality, ensuring provenance, and embedding metadata into creation processes. In data management, it prevents downstream quality problems and supports lineage and accountability. For the business, it reduces rework, improves operational efficiency, and strengthens data use cases with high-quality and trustworthy data. Topics include:

- Standards for names, formats, and allowable values
- Validation and reference checks at capture
- Provenance and context capture at entry
- Metadata collection at creation
- Responsibilities of data producers
- Upstream change management and notifications
- Interfaces and capture systems design
- Test data and privacy constraints.

Data Consumption Knowledge focuses on how data is reported, interpreted, analyzed, and applied by end users. For data stewards, it means ensuring metrics, dashboards, and reports are governed, clear, and correctly interpreted. In data management, it enables stewardship to monitor usage, provide feedback, and retire outdated assets. For the business, it shapes decisions based on consistent metrics, trusted insights, and an informed and data-literate workforce. Topics include:

- Report, dashboard, and visualization patterns and standards
- Alignment and governance of business metrics
- Data provenance and usage guidelines for consumers
- Informed and ethical interpretation practices
- Usage monitoring and feedback loops
- Self-service data access and data products
- Consumer literacy needs and training
- Retirement of outdated or unused assets.

Human and Interpersonal Knowledge

Communication Knowledge enables stewards to convey data meaning, concepts, policies, issues, and decisions clearly and effectively. For data stewards, this means tailoring messages to specific audiences, practicing active listening, and documenting decisions. In data management, it fosters transparency, accountability, and shared understanding. For the business, it fosters trust, enhances collaboration, and ensures that data-driven conversations lead to actionable outcomes. Topics include:

- Communication modes (written, verbal, and visual)
- Active listening techniques
- Explaining decisions and reasoning
- Transparency in issues, risks, and resolutions
- Communication tailored to audiences (execs versus analysts)
- Visual storytelling with data

- Channels for ongoing communication
- Documentation and decision logging.

Group Dynamics Knowledge helps individuals to guide and participate in collaborative work. For data stewards, this includes understanding team norms, managing conflict, and applying decision-making methods. This knowledge is especially valuable when stewards are called upon to facilitate discussions and workshops, and to guide groups to consensus decisions. In data management, it ensures stewardship activities benefit from balanced participation, constructive dialogue, and shared responsibility. For the business, it improves collaboration, accelerates consensus, and strengthens organizational trust in collective outcomes. Topics include:

- Team norms and ground rules
- Conflict sources and resolution strategies
- Facilitation methods (reframing and structured questions)
- Decision-making models (consent, consult, consensus, and voting)
- Participation balance and equity
- Role rotation and shared responsibility
- Trust-building in groups
- Retrospective and reflection practices.

Collaboration Knowledge underpins cross-functional stewardship efforts by guiding development of shared goals, protocols, processes, and tools for joint work. For data stewards, it means engaging stakeholders, coordinating efforts, and co-owning deliverables. In data management, it promotes alignment across governance, architecture, and operations. For the business, it enables coordinated action, reduces silos, and delivers outcomes that reflect the needs of all stakeholders. Topics include:

- Stakeholder mapping and engagement
- Shared goals and agreements
- Working agreements and protocols
- Tools and platforms for collaboration
- Co-editing and joint ownership of artifacts
- Coordination mechanisms (councils, committees, and standups)
- Knowledge-sharing practices
- Recognition and reinforcement of collaboration.

Change Management Knowledge helps to ensure that data management policies, practices, and processes are adopted, sustained, and adapted over time. For data stewards, it means planning rollouts, training, and incentives to support adoption. In data management, it embeds stewardship into evolving systems, processes, and policies. For the business, it helps with successful transitions, risks mitigation, and sustainable data value. Topics include:

- Stakeholder impact assessment
- Phased rollouts and pilots
- Communications planning
- Training and readiness activities

- Incentives and performance alignment
- Version control for policies and standards
- Feedback loops and iteration
- Adoption measurement and reporting.

Policy Compliance *Knowledge* guides understanding, interpretation, and consistent application of data management policies. For data stewards, this knowledge helps with clear interpretation of policies, and with framing of guidance that helps others apply the policies. In data management, it supports embedding policies into systems, workflows, and audits so adherence becomes part of routine operations. For the business, it reduces risk, strengthens accountability, and demonstrates credibility to regulators, partners, and customers. Topics include:

- Understanding and applying policy compliance formats (guides, guardrails, and gates)
- Using compliance enablement resources
- Managing exceptions and waiver processes
- Applying technical safeguards (access controls and authentication)
- Monitoring and reporting compliance
- Documenting audit evidence and practices
- Managing policy updates and changes
- Integrating policies with workflows and systems.

Coaching *Knowledge* helps stewards to build both individual and organizational data literacy and capabilities. At the individual level, it involves mentoring and guiding colleagues to increase their confidence and skills with data. At the organizational level, it contributes to broader cultural growth by fostering shared practices, resources, and support for responsible data use. For data stewards, it means mentoring peers, designing training, and supporting communities of practice. In data management, it helps spread stewardship practices by equipping others to apply them effectively. For the business, it raises the overall level of data literacy, improving the quality of decisions and embedding stewardship into the culture. Topics include:

- Data literacy basics (definitions, interpretation, and bias)
- Training design and delivery methods
- One-on-one and group coaching approaches
- Sandbox and lab environments for practice
- Feedback and assessment techniques
- Mentorship for stewards and data users
- Communities of practice and peer learning
- Linking literacy outcomes to decision quality.

Summary

Data stewardship knowledge is broad and multi-dimensional, spanning business insight, data expertise, and human interaction skills. No single steward is expected to have all of this knowledge at an expert level. Instead, stewardship programs succeed when knowledge is distributed across roles and when stewards work as a team, each contributing their depth of expertise while maintaining awareness of the broader landscape.

The distinction between primary and secondary knowledge is not intended to limit stewards, but to provide structure for growth and collaboration. Primary knowledge defines the essential capabilities for a given role, while secondary knowledge builds awareness, context, and the ability to connect across boundaries. Together they form a balanced foundation that strengthens both individual practice and collective stewardship.

Ultimately, stewardship knowledge matters because it turns good intentions into effective action. Knowledgeable stewards can recognize risks, shape opportunities, and guide responsible practices. Knowledgeable teams can integrate perspectives, bridge organizational divides, and sustain momentum. The impact is felt not only in the quality and trustworthiness of data, but also in the confidence of the business to rely on data as a strategic asset.

FIVE

Data Stewards as Problem Solvers

Data issues rarely present themselves with clarity. They show up as late reports, conflicting metrics, unreliable dashboards, or frustrated users who can't access the information they need. For organizations that depend on data, these problems are more than annoyances—they are risks to performance, compliance, and trust. Data stewards are often the first to recognize when something is wrong and are uniquely positioned to guide the process of resolving it. To succeed, they need more than technical fixes; they require structured approaches, problem-solving skills, and facilitation techniques that transform scattered symptoms into cohesive solutions.

A Diagnostic Guide

The Data Steward's Field Guide (included as an appendix in this book) contains a practical diagnostic tool to support problem-solving in the field. This tool helps stewards trace a path from data issues they observe—what we refer to as symptoms—through the likely causes and on to feasible solutions.

At the heart of the guide are structured tables that organize these symptoms around core data management processes. For each process, the guide presents a set of common symptoms, identifies potential root causes, and recommends actionable solutions.

To use the diagnostic tool, start by browsing the index of symptoms. This index acts as a quick entry point to locate the issues you're seeing—inconsistent definitions, poor structural integrity, limited data access, etc. Each symptom is linked to one or more process areas, where diagnostic tables provide further guidance. The diagnostic guide is more than just a reference—it's a facilitation tool. It's designed to support collaboration by engaging stakeholders in shared problem-solving. It encourages teams to align on the issues, consider root causes together, and reach agreement on solutions that are both sound and practical.

Problem-solving Skills

The diagnostic guide helps stewards recognize symptoms, trace them to root causes, and identify possible remedies. But diagnosis is only one part of the problem-solving process. Diagnosing and resolving data issues isn't just about knowing what's wrong—it's about how you approach the problem to identify and implement solutions.

The process starts with awareness—recognizing that a problem or risk exists. From there, problem solvers move to diagnosis, pinpointing specific issues. Analysis then helps uncover the root causes behind the symptoms. Once causes are understood, the focus shifts to synthesis—defining and shaping practical solutions. Data stewards rarely act alone, so facilitation plays a key role in alignment and advocacy for process and policy changes needed to implement solutions. Two complementary capabilities strengthen problem solving. Communication spans every stage, making data concepts understandable, managing expectations, and driving cultural and behavioral change. Process improvement sits at the core, using insights from diagnosis, analysis, and synthesis to address root causes and raise the maturity of data management practices across the organization. Together, they turn diagnostic insight into tangible results.

Awareness	Diagnosis	Analysis	Synthesis	Facilitation

Communication

Process Improvement

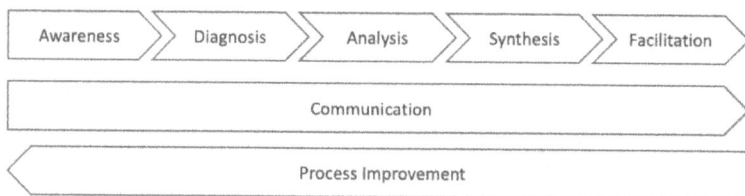

Figure 19: Problem-solving Skills for Data Stewards.

Core Data Management Processes

Now that we've seen the problem-solving skills that guide data stewardship work, let's look at 14 core data management processes where those skills are applied.

These are the functional areas where most data challenges occur and where data stewards typically focus their time and effort. The first five—naming, defining, and designing data; managing data quality; and integrating data—are geared to getting data into a usable, trusted state.

The next six—accessing data, managing metadata, managing databases, managing systems, governing data, and protecting data—support the broader technical and organizational environment that surrounds and enables effective data use.

The last three—preparing data, analyzing data, and automating with data—focus on data use itself.

Each process area includes recurring issues that can be diagnosed and resolved using the guide. Together, these processes define the scope of day-to-day data stewardship and provide the structure for navigating complex data environments.

Common Symptoms of Data Dysfunction

Symptoms are the visible signs of dysfunction—signals that something is wrong. They include incomplete data, conflicting metrics, inconsistent documentation, inaccessible systems, duplicate records, shadow copies, untraceable lineage, and much more. Nearly a hundred symptoms are cataloged in the guide. Recognizing symptoms aligns naturally with the awareness stage of problem-solving. For data stewards, recognizing symptoms is often the starting point for action, providing the first indication that further investigation is needed.

Common Causes of Data Dysfunction

Behind each symptom lies one or more causes. These are the conditions, oversights, and weaknesses that lead to recurring problems: inadequate metadata, poor quality controls, weak security, cloud misconfigurations, fragmented tools, missing standards, and lack of accountability, among others. The guide identifies about ninety such causes, linking them to the symptoms that they produce. The list supports diagnosis, helping stewards identify which issues exist so they can investigate underlying causes and guide resolution efforts. Stewards who can recognize causes are equipped to move beyond surface-level fixes and address the systemic conditions that perpetuate dysfunction.

Solutions for Data Dysfunction

Diagnosis should lead to action—causal analysis, synthesis of solutions, and putting solutions into play. The guide catalogs nearly a hundred solutions, each connected to specific causes and symptoms. Solutions span technical practices (e.g., automated deduplication and metadata repositories), process improvements (e.g., documented workflows and quality monitoring), governance mechanisms (e.g., compliance frameworks and role-based access controls), and cultural levers (e.g., executive sponsorship and literacy programs). These remedies provide practical options for stewards and stakeholders to consider when charting a path forward.

From Symptoms to Solutions

The diagnostic guide is designed to be navigated step by step: begin with the symptom index, follow links to the processes where issues occur, review the mapped causes, and select targeted solutions.

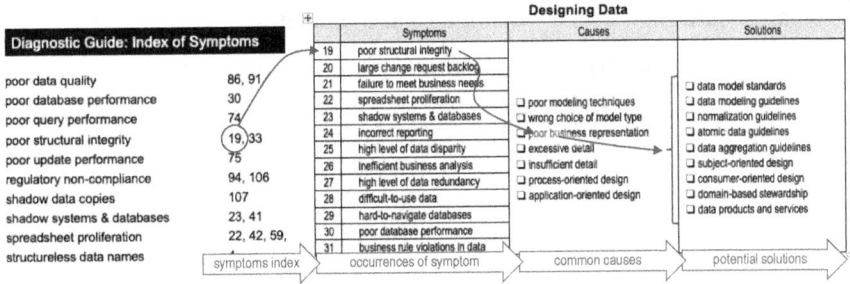

Diagnostic Guide: Index of Symptoms		Designing Data		
		Symptoms	Causes	Solutions
poor data quality	86, 91	19 poor structural integrity		❑ data model standards
poor database performance	30	20 large change request backlog		❑ data modeling guidelines
poor query performance	74	21 failure to meet business needs	❑ poor modeling techniques	❑ normalization guidelines
poor structural integrity	(19), 33	22 spreadsheet proliferation	❑ wrong choice of model type	❑ atomic data guidelines
poor update performance	75	23 shadow systems & databases	❑ poor business representation	❑ subject-oriented design
regulatory non-compliance	94, 106	24 incorrect reporting	❑ excessive detail	❑ data aggregation guidelines
shadow data copies	107	25 high level of data disparity	❑ insufficient detail	❑ consumer-oriented design
shadow systems & databases	23, 41	26 inefficient business analysis	❑ process-oriented design	❑ domain-based stewardship
spreadsheet proliferation	22, 42, 59,	27 high level of data redundancy	❑ application-oriented design	❑ data products and services
structureless data names		28 difficult-to-use data		
		29 hard-to-navigate databases		
		30 poor database performance		
		31 business rule violations in data		
	symptoms index	occurrences of symptom	common causes	potential solutions

Figure 20: From Symptoms to Solutions.

The process begins with the symptom index—an entry point for identifying observable problems. Each symptom is cross-referenced to one or more core data management processes where causes are often found. Within each process area, tables list the likely causes and offer potential solutions. This structured path—from identifying symptoms, through understanding causes, to selecting targeted remedies—helps data stewards move from reactive firefighting to proactive problem-solving with clarity and confidence.

Facilitating Collaborative Solutions

While much of the guide focuses on technical processes and structured diagnostics, problem-solving must also consider the human side of data stewardship. Solving data problems often involves facilitating discussions, aligning diverse perspectives, and building shared understanding. Participatory decision-making relies on the data steward's ability to create an inclusive environment where all voices are heard and respected. Strong interpersonal skills—such as listening, questioning, reframing, and guiding group dialogue—are essential to move from disagreement to mutual understanding and ultimately to collaborative, lasting solutions.

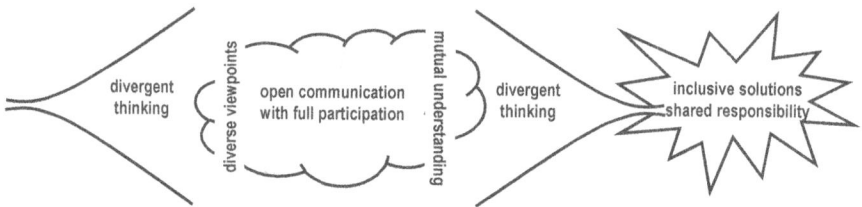

Figure 22: Facilitation and Collaborative Decision Making.

The facilitation process moves through stages, beginning with divergent thinking, where participants surface diverse viewpoints and explore possibilities without judgment. This stage depends on open communication and active participation, creating space for all perspectives to be expressed. Through dialogue and interaction, divergent ideas are gradually shaped into mutual understanding. From there, the process shifts to convergent thinking, where common ground is identified, and solutions are refined and aligned. The outcome is not just agreement but inclusive solutions with shared responsibility—results that participants both understand and own. This dynamic highlights the steward's role as facilitator, guiding the group from many voices toward unified action.

Effective facilitation requires more than simply keeping a meeting on track—it involves creating an environment where all voices are heard, ideas are explored, and consensus can emerge. The field guide includes a quick reference of several techniques for practical group facilitation. Each technique is a way to encourage participation, manage group dynamics, or structure thinking so that discussions are productive and solutions are inclusive.

Summary

Problem-solving is a large part of the day-to-day work of data stewardship. It requires more than quick fixes—it calls for structured diagnosis, disciplined analysis, and practical solutions, all guided by facilitation and communication. *The Data Steward's Field Guide* provides a framework to recognize symptoms, uncover causes, and move to solutions. It also offers tools and techniques to address the human side of transitioning from problems to solutions—group dynamics, facilitation, and collaborative problem-solving.

Six

Implementing and Evolving a Data Stewardship Program

Implementing and evolving a data stewardship program requires more than appointing a few individuals to steward data. It requires a deliberate effort that combines leadership commitment, guiding principles, teamwork, and sustained investment. A stewardship program operates at the intersection of business and data, which means it must reflect both strategic direction from executives and practical realities of day-to-day data management and use. Establishing the program involves defining roles, aligning with governance, and building processes and structures that scale over time. Equally important, stewardship must be embedded into organizational culture—so that accountability, collaboration, and continuous improvement become part of how people approach data in their daily work.

Executive Sponsorship

Implementing and evolving a data stewardship program begins with executive commitment. Active sponsorship from senior leaders, such as a CIO, CDO, or CEO, lays the foundation for long-term success. That commitment means more than just funding the program. It's about aligning stewardship with business strategy, making it visible and credible across the enterprise, and providing the tools, people, and time needed to make it work. Strong executive support also reinforces accountability structures and drives cultural change by setting expectations and modeling the value of data responsibility from the top down.

Guiding Principles for Data Stewardship

A successful data stewardship program needs more than good intentions—it needs a solid foundation of guiding principles that steer actions and decisions. These principles serve as best practices, ensuring that stewardship efforts are aligned with business needs, regulatory expectations, and the realities of day-to-day data management and use. Effective data stewardship programs are developed and operated with these principles in mind:

- **Accountability,** where clearly defined roles establish stewards as answerable for how data is managed, protected, and used.

- **Data quality** as a central goal, focusing on correctness, integrity, usability, and objectivity—qualities that build trust and support the continuum of data uses from basic reporting to advanced AI use cases.

- **Transparency** makes data management processes and data governance decisions visible. Stakeholders understand how and why data is used and why it is controlled.

- **Compliance and Ethics** principles guide alignment with regulations and standards and reinforce objectives of responsible and respectful data use.

- **Security and Privacy** safeguard sensitive information from unauthorized access or misuse—an essential function in today's data landscape.

- **Accessibility and Usability** make data easy to find and understand, while balancing access security controls.

- **Lifecycle Management** emphasizes the importance of sustainable practices throughout the whole data journey, from creation to deletion.

- **Collaboration and Culture** principles remind us that good stewardship depends on shared values, human engagement, cooperation, and active participation across the organization.

- **Data as an Enterprise Asset** reinforces the idea that data belongs to the whole organization—not individuals or departments—and stewardship exists to protect and grow its value.

- **Embedded Stewardship** principles position stewardship responsibilities as part of everyday work, not side tasks or afterthoughts, and not as an external controlling body.

- **Continuous Improvement** ensures that stewardship implementation isn't a one-time effort. Processes, standards, and practices are regularly reviewed to ensure adaptation and improvement.

- **Stakeholder Education** helps everyone involved in data—creators, consumers, owners, governors, custodians, and stewards—understand their roles and act competently.

- **User-Centric Mindset** focuses stewardship on improving data usability and the user experience— making data easier to find, understand, and access, and supporting frictionless interactions.

- **Building Trust** is a cornerstone of stewardship that strives to make data reliable, understandable, and usable, and also to make data policies and processes understandable and transparent.

- **Stewardship by Example** positions stewards to shape culture through their actions—they model effective practices that others can follow.

- **Stewardship as Service** grounds the program in its purpose: to serve the business and protect people by ensuring data is used appropriately, effectively, and fairly.

Stewardship is a Team Job

Data stewardship is a big job—too big for anyone to do alone. Implementing and sustaining a strong stewardship program calls for a team approach. That's because data stewards are expected to take many kinds of actions, fulfill a wide variety of roles, have deep and broad knowledge across data domains, and use well-developed human skills.

No single person is likely to bring all of that to the table. The work of stewardship includes advising, guiding, coordinating, coaching, and remediating problems—actions that require both initiative and collaboration. Stewards assume roles such as facilitator, communicator, influencer, and problem solver—each one essential, yet demanding in its own way. To perform these roles effectively, stewards must be knowledgeable about a broad spectrum of data management topics—data quality, data access, metadata management, integration, interoperability, ethics, governance, and much more. Equally important, stewards rely heavily on interpersonal skills: communication, collaboration, consensus-building, decision-making, and the ability to work as part of a team.

> *Stewardship isn't a solo act. It takes a team, bringing together complementary skills, shared responsibility, and a commitment to working together. That's how data stewardship succeeds.*

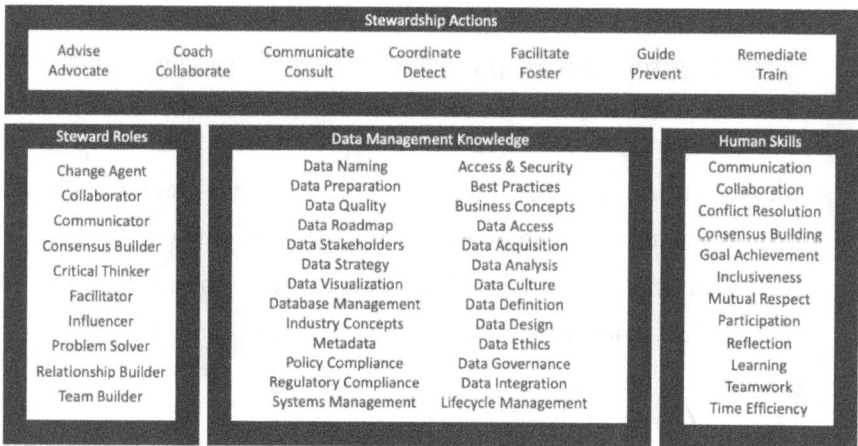

Stewardship Actions						
Advise Advocate	Coach Collaborate	Communicate Consult	Coordinate Detect	Facilitate Foster	Guide Prevent	Remediate Train

Steward Roles	Data Management Knowledge		Human Skills
Change Agent Collaborator Communicator Consensus Builder Critical Thinker Facilitator Influencer Problem Solver Relationship Builder Team Builder	Data Naming Data Preparation Data Quality Data Roadmap Data Stakeholders Data Strategy Data Visualization Database Management Industry Concepts Metadata Policy Compliance Regulatory Compliance Systems Management	Access & Security Best Practices Business Concepts Data Access Data Acquisition Data Analysis Data Culture Data Definition Data Design Data Ethics Data Governance Data Integration Lifecycle Management	Communication Collaboration Conflict Resolution Consensus Building Goal Achievement Inclusiveness Mutual Respect Participation Reflection Learning Teamwork Time Efficiency

It is not realistic or practical to expect one individual to excel in all of these areas.

Data Stewardship is clearly a **TEAM** job!

Figure 23: Stewardship Is a Team Job.

Data Stewardship Teams

Data stewardship functions most effectively when it operates in two complementary modes: a collaborative peer team and a formal governance structure. These aren't alternative approaches but concurrent and interconnected ones. Every data steward plays a role in both. The stewardship team, as a peer-driven, cross-functional group, works horizontally across the organization, bringing together stewards who are responsible for subject areas, business units, processes, and projects. As a team, their focus is on shared goals—ensuring data quality, resolving issues, clarifying definitions, and supporting day-to-day data needs. The expectation in this structure is active collaboration, knowledge sharing, and mutual support. Peer accountability and informal leadership dynamics are central to its function.

Data stewards, both individually and as teams, are also part of the broader data governance team. The more formal structure of data governance brings alignment with the CDO and other executives, the Data Governance Council, and enterprise-wide standards and policies. In this structure, individual stewards are expected to represent their domain, contribute to governance decisions, and ensure that stewardship practices align with enterprise strategy. There is a clear chain of accountability and defined authority.

These two structures operate in parallel. Peer teams focus on execution, getting stewardship work done collaboratively and responsively. The governance structure provides guidance, oversight, and alignment with business priorities. Stewards navigate both, moving between collaborative coordination and formal reporting. This dual role requires agility, as it involves contributing to the team while also fulfilling governance responsibilities. When both dimensions work in harmony, the result is a stewardship program that is both responsive and strategic.

Staffing the Stewardship Organization

Staffing the data stewardship organization involves balancing organizational needs with available resources, often by blending part-time and full-time roles. The choice depends on factors such as company size, data complexity, regulatory requirements, and the maturity of the stewardship program. Part-time data stewards are common in smaller organizations or those that are just beginning their data stewardship efforts. In these cases, stewardship is added as a role (not a job title) alongside existing responsibilities. To be successful, this approach requires shifting priorities, setting clear expectations, and providing support through training and tools. It fits well in distributed governance environments where stewardship duties are shared across many contributors. Full-time data stewards are more common in larger, more mature organizations with complex data landscapes or stringent regulatory requirements. These roles are formalized within the organization, with well-defined job descriptions, clear performance goals, and established reporting structures. Full-time stewards bring dedicated focus to data issues and help drive consistency and accountability across the enterprise.

Most organizations operate with a mix of full-time and part-time stewards. For example, an enterprise steward may be a full-time role responsible for overseeing the stewardship collaborative stewardship team, while business stewards, subject stewards, and process stewards may serve in part-time capacities embedded within business units or operational functions. Project stewards often serve in short-term roles, providing stewardship for the duration of a specific initiative or transformation effort. This flexible approach enables organizations to align stewardship responsibilities with both strategic needs and practical realities, and to adapt and adjust as needs evolve.

Data Stewardship Roadmap

Developing a data stewardship program takes time, planning, and a phased approach. A practical roadmap outlines a realistic path to build and evolve such a program, striking a balance between initial setup activities and ongoing operational work.

The early months focus on foundational steps: defining the vision and objectives to clarify purpose and scope, assessing the current state of data to identify needs, and establishing stewardship roles and responsibilities. These steps create the organizational alignment necessary for long-term success.

Roadmap Phase	Timeline	Activities
Vision and Objectives	1-2 months	Define purpose, scope, and key stakeholders
Data Assessment	1-3 months	Conduct data inventory and gap analysis
Stewardship Roles	2-3 months	Appoint stewards, define roles and responsibilities
Governance Framework	2-4 months	Develop policies, standards, and access controls
Quality and Compliance	3-4 months	Establish quality management and compliance processes
Tools and Infrastructure	4-6 months	Implement essential data cataloging, quality, and metadata tools
Training and Education	Ongoing	Provide training for data stewards, owners, creators, and consumers
Stewardship Activities	Ongoing	Data quality monitoring, issue resolution, access control audits, policy management, and much more
Monitoring and Improvement	Ongoing	Continuously review stewardship effectiveness and adjust as needed
Scaling and Evolution	Ongoing	Adapt to new challenges and grow the program as the stewardship organization expands and matures

Table 2: Data Stewardship Roadmap.

Next comes the governance framework, which involves developing policies, standards, access controls, quality processes, and compliance processes to provide data that is trustworthy and well-managed. Implementing supporting tools and infrastructure rounds out the setup phase, enabling stewards to catalog data, track quality, and manage metadata. Several workstreams continue on an ongoing basis. Training and education is needed to build steward and stakeholder capabilities and keep pace with change. Stewardship activities such as audits, issue resolution, and access reviews are part of daily operations. Monitoring and improvement activities help the program to be responsive and effective. And as the organization grows or faces new challenges, stewardship must scale and evolve to meet changing needs. Keep in mind that the roadmap shown in table 2 is just an example. It should be adapted to reflect your organization's unique needs, priorities, and resources. Factors such as organizational maturity, data complexity, compliance demands, and available staffing will all influence how and when activities take place. Most importantly, treat the roadmap as a living plan. Just as data and business needs evolve, so too will stewardship goals. Ongoing planning and periodic adjustments are necessary to ensure the program continues to deliver value over time.

Data Stewardship Metrics and KPIs

Metrics and KPIs play a central role in evaluating the success of a data stewardship program. They make the work of stewards visible, measurable, and actionable. They transform stewardship from a set of good intentions into a results-driven discipline. These measures help identify what's working well, where improvements are needed, and how stewardship efforts contribute to business and data outcomes. Several categories of metrics reflect the broad scope of data stewardship responsibilities:

- Data quality metrics track the condition of the data itself, such as accuracy, completeness, and timeliness.

- Efficiency metrics assess how well stewards are able to manage tasks and resolve issues.

- Governance compliance metrics monitor adherence to data policies and standards.

- Other categories address access and usage patterns, data security, and the adoption of stewardship practices by the broader organization.

As you design metrics for your stewardship program, align them closely with your organization's goals and priorities. Choose metrics that provide meaningful feedback, support accountability, and guide program improvement. Most importantly, treat measurement as a dynamic activity, refining metrics over time to reflect evolving objectives, new challenges, and lessons learned from experience.

Data Stewardship Maturity

The data stewardship maturity model illustrates how data stewardship evolves from informal, ad hoc efforts to a fully integrated and strategically aligned discipline. It highlights not only the stages of growth, but also the characteristics that define each stage and the kinds of progress organizations can aim for.

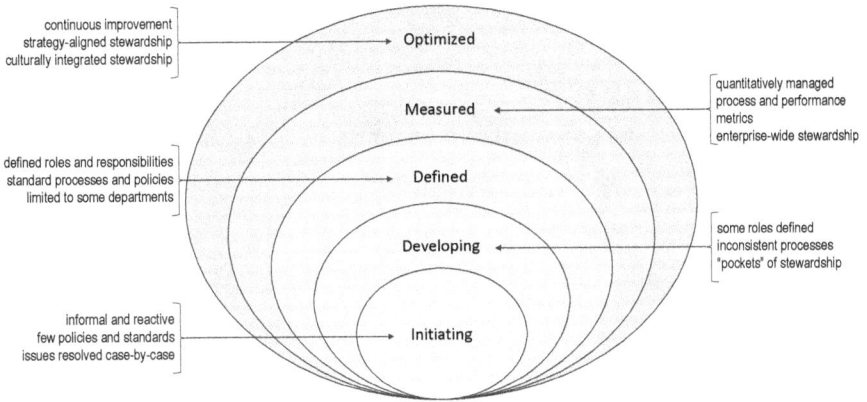

Figure 24: The Data Stewardship Maturity Model.

Organizations typically begin at the Initiating stage, where stewardship is reactive and handled case-by-case with few formal policies. As they move into the Developing stage, they begin to define roles and processes, though efforts are often inconsistent and limited to isolated teams or projects. In the Defined stage, stewardship becomes more structured—roles, responsibilities and policies are documented and adopted more broadly, though often still department-focused. Reaching the Measured stage means stewardship is established across the enterprise, with processes monitored using metrics and performance indicators. Finally, the Optimized stage reflects a culture of continuous improvement, where stewardship is aligned with business strategy and embedded into the organization's values and operations. This model is not just a way to assess current state—it also provides a framework for progress and continuous evolution. It can help identify improvement opportunities, support planning efforts and set realistic expectations for building a mature and sustainable stewardship program.

Summary

A successful data stewardship program doesn't remain static. It begins with executive sponsorship, guiding principles, and immediate needs. It matures through practice, iteration, and continuous alignment with business needs. Teams play a central role, balancing collaborative problem-solving with formal governance responsibilities, while staffing models adapt to organizational size, maturity, and complexity. Roadmaps provide direction, but flexibility supports responsiveness to change. Metrics make stewardship visible and measurable, while maturity models guide progress toward integration and optimization. Most importantly, stewardship evolves as both a discipline and a culture. When supported and nurtured, it becomes embedded in the way the organization operates, ensuring that data remains trustworthy, well-managed, and positioned to deliver value well into the future.

The Data Steward's Field Guide

The Data Steward's Field Guide is built as a quick, practical reference for anyone with the responsibilities of data stewardship. It brings together essential tools, techniques, and diagnostic aids that stewards can rely on to recognize problems, understand causes, and move toward solutions that strengthen data management and governance.

Use it as a working companion. The diagnostic section helps you start with the symptoms you observe in your data and trace them to their root causes, providing clear options for resolution. The facilitation section offers methods to guide conversations, encourage participation, and foster a shared understanding. Whether you are addressing data quality issues, integration challenges, or governance discussions, the guide is designed to keep stewards effective, focused, and ready to act.

This guide is protected by copyright (© 2025 by Dave Wells). But the purpose is to advance the practice of data stewardship as a profession. The guide is useful only if it is distributed and applied. With that goal in mind, I grant permission to copy, reproduce, and distribute the document as widely as is needed for non-commercial uses to further the practice and disciplines of data stewardship. You may not reproduce for resale or for-profit endeavors—only for internal use in your organization's data stewardship efforts.

Wishing you data stewardship success.

Dave Wells

dwells@infocentric.org

What Does a Data Steward Do?

As a data steward, you'll find that your responsibilities span across time—looking to the past, engaging with the present, and anticipating the future. Each timeframe offers a unique lens through which your work adds value, and each demands a different emphasis on the core activities you perform.

The matrix below outlines five key activities: identifying issues, alleviating symptoms, remediating problems, mitigating risks, and facilitating solutions. While you'll engage in all of these throughout your role, their relevance and intensity vary depending on whether you're reflecting on what has already happened, managing current realities, or planning for what lies ahead. For example, identifying issues is essential across all timeframes, but remediation is especially critical in the present. Looking to the future, your focus will shift more toward mitigating risks and facilitating long-term solutions that promote growth and maturity for data governance and data management.

Understanding how your work flexes across time helps you stay proactive, prioritize effectively, and ensures that your stewardship drives both immediate impact and sustained improvement.

	Identify Issues	Alleviate Symptoms	Remediate Problems	Mitigate Risks	Facilitate Solutions
Past	✗	✗			
Present	✗	✗	✗	✗	✗
Future	✗	✗	✗	✗	✗

Key Data Steward Skills

Developing and using the right skill set is essential to navigating the complexities of data stewardship. The diagram below outlines the key skills you'll draw on throughout your work, moving from awareness to facilitation in a progression that reflects how problems are surfaced, understood, and ultimately addressed. This isn't a one-time path—it's a cycle you'll revisit often as data challenges evolve.

You begin by building awareness—recognizing when something isn't quite right. From there, you move into diagnosis, where you pinpoint the nature and scope of the issue. Analysis helps to dig deeper into root causes, while synthesis focuses on defining viable solutions. Ultimately, facilitation empowers you to advocate for change and support its effective implementation. Supporting these efforts are two foundational capabilities: communication, which underpins ability to engage stakeholders and influence behavior, and process improvement, supporting stewardship contributions to data management maturity and lasting organizational value.

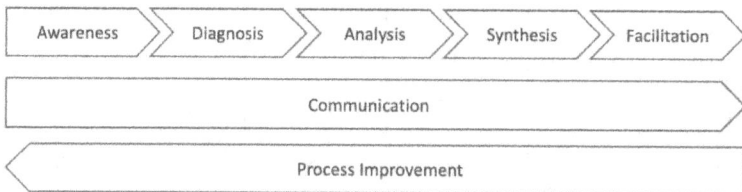

Figure 21: Problem-solving Skills for Data Stewards.

- Awareness (recognition of problems and risks)
- Diagnosis (identification of problems and risks)
- Analysis (understanding of root causes)
- Synthesis (definition of solutions)
- Facilitation (project advocacy and process change)

- Communication (data literacy and competencies, behavioral and cultural change)
- Process Improvement (data management maturity).

Facilitation Guide

Data stewards are often called upon to lead or support conversations that influence how data is defined, managed, and used. Whether you're guiding a working session, moderating a discussion, or helping a group reach a decision, effective facilitation is key to creating a productive and inclusive environment.

This guide provides a quick reference to help you prepare for and navigate facilitation responsibilities. It outlines core facilitator goals, highlights the difference between typical and participatory group dynamics, and offers a variety of techniques you can use to encourage engagement, manage disagreement, and support thoughtful decision-making.

Use this section as a practical toolkit, something you can return to whenever you need to foster clarity, collaboration, and shared ownership in data-related discussions.

Full Participation	All key stakeholders participate
	All participants actively engaged
Mutual Understanding	Seeing through the eyes of others
	Appreciation for all perspectives
Inclusive Solutions	Collaboratively developed
	Consensus based
Shared Responsibility	Mutual trust
	Mutual accountability
Ethical Deliberation	Responsible use explicitly considered
	Values and consequences considered

Table 2: Facilitator Goals.

Decision Process

Understanding the three stages of group decision-making is helpful when facilitating decision-making processes. Divergent thinking generates diverse viewpoints and ideas. Open communication with full participation builds mutual understanding among participants. Convergent thinking brings perspectives together to reach inclusive solutions with shared responsibility.

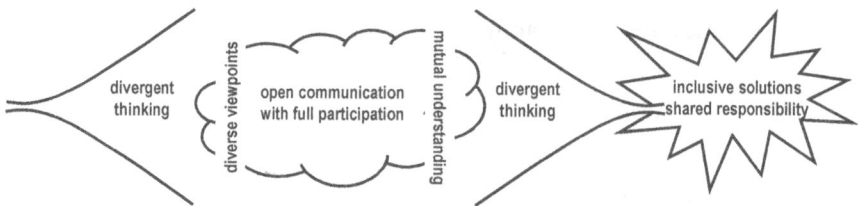

Figure 22: Facilitation and Collaborative Decision Making.

Typical Group	Participatory Group
Most vocal, articulate, and confident dominate conversations and are the most heard.	Everyone is heard, not just the loudest and most persistent. Quiet people are encouraged to speak up.
Different points of view are seen as "conflict" that must be resolved or eliminated.	Different points of view are the tools of lively discussion and full understanding.
Questioning is perceived as challenging, refuting, and creating conflict.	Questioning is encouraged as the means by which mutual understanding is achieved.
People stop listening, tune out, or focus on what they'll say next	Listeners pay attention, confident that they'll have the opportunity to be heard.
Some people close up and avoid speaking on controversial subjects.	Controversy without conflict is possible. All participants make their positions known.
Side conversations and outside-the-group maneuvers lead to divisiveness.	Out-of-group and behind-the-back discussion is discouraged as a harmful practice.
Minority viewpoints are often overrun by the voice of the majority.	Minority viewpoints are encouraged, heard, and recognized as valuable contributions.
Decisions are driven by the majority viewpoint, the most vocal, or the most powerful.	Decisions are reached when everyone who is affected understands the reasoning.

Table 3: Group Dynamics.

Facilitation Techniques

Effective facilitation requires more than simply keeping a meeting on track—it involves creating an environment where all voices are heard, ideas are explored, and consensus can emerge. The techniques in this quick reference provide practical tools to support those goals. Each method offers a way to encourage participation, manage group dynamics, or structure thinking so that discussions remain productive and inclusive.

Open Questions	Questions designed to spark discussion by encouraging elaboration, not "yes/no" answers.
Icebreakers	Quick, lighthearted prompts or activities that help participants relax, build rapport, and orient to the collaboration session
Reframing	Shifting the way a problem is presented or understood to open up new perspectives or solution paths.
Restatement	The facilitator paraphrases a participant's comment to clarify meaning and ensure shared understanding.
Parking Lot	Capturing off-topic or future-relevant ideas in a visible space to keep the discussion focused while respecting those contributions.
Brainstorming	A creativity tool where participants freely generate many ideas without judgment.
Concept Fan / Mind Map	A visual branching diagram that starts with a central idea and radiates outward into related subtopics or solutions.
Blue Sky	Encouraging participants to think wildly or without constraints—"anything is possible"—to explore innovative ideas.
Anonymous Index Cards	Participants write ideas privately and submit them without attribution, which can surface candid or less common perspectives.
Red–Yellow–Green	A quick color-coded feedback method. Participants have colored cards that they can place in front of them to provide sentiment feedback without interrupting. Red = Disagree, Yellow = Uncertain/Confused, Green = Agree.
Deferred Judgment	Postponing critique or evaluation of ideas until after generation, to keep creativity flowing without premature filtering.
Role Reversal	Asking participants to argue or think from another stakeholder's perspective or role to broaden empathy and insight.
Simulation	Role-playing or scenario enactments that let participants test ideas or decisions in a dynamic, experiential context.

Open Questions	Questions designed to spark discussion by encouraging elaboration, not "yes/no" answers.
Facts versus Assumptions	Clarifying what is known versus what is taken for granted or guessed, helping groups ground discussions on evidence and reveal biases
Six Hats	A structured "parallel thinking" model where participants take on six distinct thinking modes (e.g., facts, emotions, creativity, pessimism, optimism, and process control) to explore an issue collaboratively and systematically: • White Hat—Facts and Information: Focus on data, evidence, and objective information. • Red Hat—Feelings and Intuition: Express emotions, gut reactions, and intuitive insights. • Black Hat—Caution and Risks: Identify potential problems, weaknesses, and dangers. • Yellow Hat—Benefits and Optimism: Highlight advantages, opportunities, and positive outcomes. • Green Hat—Creativity and Alternatives: Generate new ideas, possibilities, and innovative approaches. • Blue Hat—Process and Control: Manage the thinking process itself—set focus, summarize, and direct the flow.

Table 4: Facilitation Techniques.

Diagnostic Guide

This guide is designed to help data stewards diagnose and address common kinds of data dysfunction by organizing them around the core data management processes where the root causes are most likely to be found. The fourteen core data management tasks span from basic tasks like naming and defining data to more complex activities such as governing, analyzing, and automating with data.

Core Data Management Processes

- Naming Data
- Defining Data
- Designing Data
- Managing Data Quality
- Integrating Data
- Accessing Data
- Managing Metadata

- Managing Databases
- Managing Systems
- Governing Data
- Protecting Data
- Preparing Data
- Analyzing Data
- Automating with Data

What follows is a set of diagnostic tables—one for each process. Each table includes three columns: (1) Symptoms you might observe in the data, (2) Likely causes linked to that process, and (3) Recommended solutions that address those root issues.

The purpose is to trace visible problems (such as incorrect data names or high data disparity) back to the underlying process issues (such as lack of standards or informal practices), and then take targeted action. An accompanying symptom index ties specific problems back to the relevant processes, helping you navigate this guide based on what you're seeing in your environment. Begin by browsing the index to find symptoms that you're experiencing. Then use the numbers in the index to find guidance in the tables.

This is a tool to support your problem-solving, equipping you to not only spot issues, but to understand why they're happening and how to fix them at the source.

Naming Data

	Symptoms	Causes	Solutions
1	meaningless data names	❏ informal naming practices ❏ lack of naming standards ❏ standards non-compliance ❏ data naming in acquired systems	❏ data naming taxonomy ❏ data naming vocabulary ❏ standard naming structure ❏ standard abbreviations list ❏ compliance incentives ❏ semantic data model
2	non-unique data names		
3	incorrect data names		
4	structureless data names		
5	confusing abbreviations		
6	multiple names and aliases		
7	unnamed data components		
8	hard-to-identify data		
9	high level of data disparity		

Defining Data

	Symptoms	Causes	Solutions
10	lack of data definitions	❏ lack of data definition standards ❏ poor data definition practices ❏ lack of business participation ❏ legacy databases ❏ disparate metadata ❏ multiple and disparate data catalogs	❏ data definition standards ❏ data definition templates ❏ business/tech collaboration ❏ data definition reviews ❏ metadata repository ❏ data catalog ❏ domain-based stewardship ❏ business glossary ❏ semantic data model
11	incorrect data definitions		
12	meaningless data definitions		
13	obsolete data definitions		
14	hard to find data definitions		
15	misunderstood data		
16	inappropriate use of data		
17	high level of data disparity		
18	high level of data redundancy		

Designing Data

	Symptoms	Causes	Solutions
19	poor structural integrity	❏ poor modeling techniques ❏ wrong choice of model type ❏ poor business representation ❏ excessive detail ❏ insufficient detail ❏ process-oriented design ❏ application-oriented design	❏ data model standards ❏ data modeling guidelines ❏ normalization guidelines ❏ atomic data guidelines ❏ data aggregation guidelines ❏ subject-oriented design ❏ consumer-oriented design ❏ domain-based stewardship ❏ data products and services
20	large change request backlog		
21	failure to meet business needs		
22	spreadsheet proliferation		
23	shadow systems and databases		
24	incorrect reporting		
25	high level of data disparity		
26	inefficient business analysis		
27	high level of data redundancy		
28	difficult-to-use data		
29	hard-to-navigate databases		
30	poor database performance		
31	business rule violations in data		

Managing Data Quality

	Symptoms	Causes	Solutions
32	lack of trust	❏ poorly defined DQ rules ❏ missing DQ rules ❏ lack of quality measures ❏ lack of quality reporting ❏ lack of accountability ❏ incomplete/incorrect edits	❏ DQ rules taxonomy ❏ well-defined DQ rules ❏ data contracts ❏ DQ metrics and measures ❏ published DQ reports ❏ DQ scorecard ❏ regular DQ audits ❏ designated DQ accountability ❏ DQ tasks in project plans ❏ observability tools ❏ data bias detection
33	poor structural integrity		
34	incorrect data		
35	untimely data		
36	incomplete data		
37	difficult-to-use data		
38	incorrect reporting		
39	inefficient business analysis		
40	business rule violations in data		
41	shadow systems and databases		
42	spreadsheet proliferation		

Integrating Data

	Symptoms	Causes	Solutions
43	high level of data disparity	❏ poor integration architecture	❏ sound integration architecture
44	overlapping and conflicting data	❏ technology-driven integration	❏ business-driven integration
45	untraceable data	❏ lack of master data management	❏ APIs, data services and products
46	enterprise reporting difficulty	❏ lack of APIs, services and products	❏ integration best practices
47	application integration difficulty	❏ poor integration practices	❏ data sourcing standards and criteria
48	complex system interfaces	❏ missing or wrong data sources	❏ data lineage tracking
49	limited data sharing		❏ semantic interoperability
50	spreadsheet proliferation		

Accessing Data

	Symptoms	Causes	Solutions
51	hard to find needed data		❏ robust metadata
52	can't access needed data	❏ missing metadata	❏ well-managed data catalog
53	data privacy compromised	❏ lack of data catalog	❏ data curation best practices
54	data security compromised	❏ missing or ineffective data curation	❏ indexing and search capabilities
55	data protections compromised	❏ insufficient indexing	❏ user-friendly tools and interfaces
56	needed access not authorized	❏ inadequate search capabilities	❏ data virtualization
57	obsolete permissions still active	❏ poor user interface	❏ service level accountability
58	data not available when needed	❏ database complexity	❏ access authorization procedures
59	hard-to-navigate databases	❏ ineffective data security processes	❏ self-service data capabilities
60	poor data access performance	❏ excessive downtime	
61	spreadsheet proliferation	❏ authorization barriers	

Managing Metadata

	Symptoms	Causes	Solutions
62	missing documentation	❏ casual metadata management	
63	incomplete documentation	❏ lack of data catalog	❏ metadata templates and guidelines
64	conflicting documentation	❏ fragmented metadata tools	
65	hard to find documentation		❏ well-managed data catalog
66	outdated documentation	❏ lack of documentation standards	❏ metadata integration tools
67	confusing documentation	❏ undocumented changes	❏ automated metadata capture
68	untraceable data	❏ no documentation incentives	❏ project documentation standards
69	misunderstood data	❏ no documentation reviews	❏ metadata accountability
70	high level of data disparity	❏ no documentation accountability	❏ metadata tasks in project plans
71	high level of data redundancy	❏ "rush to production" projects	❏ incentives and reviews

Managing Databases

	Symptoms	Causes	Solutions
72	insufficient data storage capacity	❏ ineffective storage management	❏ continuous capacity planning
73	unanticipated growth problems	❏ passive growth management	❏ proactive growth management
74	poor query performance	❏ ineffective performance tuning	❏ performance SLAs
75	poor update performance	❏ unscheduled maintenance	❏ availability and uptime SLAs
76	excessive database downtime	❏ inadequate database connectivity	❏ connection protocol standards
77	unreliable database connections	❏ insufficient backup and recovery	❏ database connectors
78	needed features not implemented	❏ cloud misconfigurations	❏ routine DBMS upgrades
79	corrupted data can't be repaired		❏ backup and recovery best practices
80	lost data can't be recovered		❏ configuration baselines and audits

Managing Systems

	Symptoms	Causes	Solutions
81	complex system interfaces	❑ poor data sharing architecture	❑ application architecture standards
82	untraceable data		❑ semantic layer
83	poor application performance	❑ lack of data integration ❑ lack of data interoperability	❑ application architecture standards
84	high level of data redundancy	❑ poor application design	❑ application design reviews
85	high level of data disparity	❑ "quick fix" maintenance	❑ maintenance and testing standards
86	poor data quality	❑ "misfit" acquired systems	
87	inadequate metadata	❑ inconsistent data formats	❑ data sharing incentives
88	data security compromised	❑ little reuse of data functions	❑ APIs, data services and products
89	data privacy compromised	❑ testing with production data	❑ managed test data and test cases
90	business rule violations in data		

Governing Data

	Symptoms	Causes	Solutions
91	poor data quality	❑ lack of data management goals	❑ "data as an asset" culture
92	data security compromised		❑ "data as a resource" culture
93	data privacy compromised	❑ poorly defined responsibilities	❑ focus on data literacy
94	regulatory non-compliance	❑ unclear or ambiguous authority	❑ designated data ownership
95	disaster recovery uncertainties	❑ poorly defined accountabilities	❑ well-defined responsibilities
96	territorialism inhibits data sharing	❑ inadequate policy management	❑ compliance frameworks
97	data retention/disposal uncertainty	❑ lack of policy compliance	❑ clearly designated authority
98	data consolidation difficulties	❑ regulatory complexity	❑ clearly defined accountabilities
99	data ownership conflicts	❑ understaffed data management	❑ executive data literacy
100	need for data standardization	❑ underfunded data management	❑ executive data sponsorship

Protecting Data

	Symptoms	Causes	Solutions
101	unauthorized data access	❏ weak access controls ❏ over-privileged user accounts ❏ poorly defined data classification ❏ insufficient logging and monitoring ❏ weak backup/recovery ❏ lack of accountability and training ❏ weak third party controls ❏ uncontrolled exports and sharing ❏ fragmented incident response	❏ role-based access control ❏ least privilege access policies ❏ data classification framework ❏ audit trails and automated monitoring ❏ encryption and tokenization ❏ compliance monitoring ❏ centralized incident response
102	unmonitored data usage		
103	data loss incidents		
104	misuse of data incidents		
105	third party data leakage		
106	regulatory non-compliance		
107	shadow data copies		
108	inability to track data breaches		
109	data privacy compromised		
110	data protections compromised		

Preparing Data

	Symptoms	Causes	Solutions
111	inconsistent data formats	❏ no data prep workflow standards ❏ poor quality source data ❏ informal / ad hoc data integration ❏ unclear data semantics ❏ lack of data understanding ❏ metadata deficiencies ❏ poor documentation practices	❏ pipeline workflow standards ❏ data profiling and validation rules ❏ automated deduplication ❏ semantic data model ❏ automated metadata capture ❏ data observability ❏ data quality monitoring ❏ documentation standards
112	missing or incomplete data		
113	duplicate records		
114	untraceable data lineage		
115	data outliers and anomalies		
116	excessive manual effort		
117	undocumented transformations		
118	unverified data sources		

Analyzing Data

	Symptoms	Causes	Solutions
119	inconsistent analysis results	❑ inconsistent metrics definitions	❑ business glossary
120	misinterpreted metrics	❑ missing semantic layer	❑ semantic layer
121	conflicting analytical models	❑ excessive use of spreadsheets	❑ repeatable analysis workflows
122	excessive manual effort	❑ undocumented analysis methods	❑ model validation and peer review
123	difficulty reproducing results	❑ limited analytic model governance	❑ documented analysis methods
124	lack of trust	❑ insufficient validation of results	❑ analysis process transparency
125	data or model bias		❑ bias detection methods
126	unverified data sources		

Automating with Data

	Symptoms	Causes	Solutions
127	automation fails if data changes	❑ schema-dependent scripts	❑ schema-flexible design
128	inconsistent automation results	❑ insufficient testing of workflows	❑ workflow testing and validation
129	excessive manual effort	❑ manual exception handling	❑ automated triage of exceptions
130	hidden dependencies	❑ semantic misalignment	❑ semantic layer
131	data or model bias	❑ weak or missing AI governance	❑ AI/ML model governance
132	decision rule drift	❑ lack of performance metrics	❑ performance monitoring
133	lack of transparency	❑ inadequate documentation	❑ documentation standards
134	monitoring and audit difficulties	❑ lack of bias detection and controls	❑ automated bias detection

Index of Symptoms

Index